National Collection of Fine Arts
Smithsonian Institution
October 19, 1967 through January 1, 1968

The Cleveland Museum of Art
Cleveland, Ohio
January 24 through March 10, 1968

The Art Galleries
University of California at Los Angeles
Los Angeles, California
April 7 through May 19, 1968

GEORGE CALEB BINGHAM 1811-1879

Catalog published for the
National Collection of Fine Arts by
Smithsonian Institution Press
Washington, D.C.

The catalog of paintings and drawings and the chronology in
this publication are derived from the forthcoming books by E. Maurice Bloch
George Caleb Bingham: The Evolution of an Artist and companion *Catalogue Raisonné*,
with the kind permission of the publisher,
the University of California Press.

Smithsonian Publication 4725

Introduction

Interest in the work of George Caleb Bingham and recognition of his importance have mounted steadily in recent years, but there have been few opportunities to form any comprehensive view of the artist without traveling to Missouri. The present exhibition brings his work to major areas of the country where it has not been seen in depth. The National Collection of Fine Arts is pleased to have been able to gather these pictures for viewers in the national capital, Ohio, and California. In this connection, we are particularly happy to have the collaboration of the Cleveland Museum of Art and of the Art Galleries of the University of California at Los Angeles.

This is the first Bingham exhibition to travel to the far West, and it is the first to come to the east coast since The Museum of Modern Art show in 1935. Even for those viewers who recall that exhibition, the present selection will present a fresh view of the artist's work, for it brings a number of his portraits into juxtaposition with his genre scenes, and it rounds out the perspective of his work with a comprehensive group of drawings.

For the selection of works, the historical notes on works exhibited and on the artist, and for the illuminating essay which follows, we wish to thank Professor E. Maurice Bloch. For the comprehensiveness of the exhibition and the pleasure it affords, we must express thanks to the lenders, especially since the owners of Bingham's works are faced with many demands on their generosity.

The wider appreciation of Bingham's stature as an artist traces back to the reappraisals and discoveries of the twenties and thirties, but it continues long after the limited enthusiasms of the "American Scene" school have faded away. His pictures remain prime sources of self-knowledge for the America of today. As time passes, our appreciation of them grows, both for the perspective they afford on our culture and society, and for the qualities of form and expression that reveal an exceptional artist.

DIRECTOR
David W. Scott
NATIONAL COLLECTION OF FINE ARTS

Lenders to the Exhibition

Mrs. William Perrin Bowdry
Dallas, Texas

The Brooklyn Museum
Brooklyn, New York

Cincinnati Art Museum
Cincinnati, Ohio

City Art Museum of St. Louis
St. Louis, Missouri

The Corcoran Gallery of Art
Washington, D.C.

Mr. and Mrs. Leslie Cowan
Columbia, Missouri

The Detroit Institute of Arts
Detroit, Michigan

Mr. and Mrs. Marshall Field
Chicago, Illinois

Hirschl & Adler Galleries, Inc.
New York, New York

Kansas City Public Library
Kansas City, Missouri

John S. Kebabian
Scarsdale, New York

Kennedy Galleries, Inc.
New York, New York

Los Angeles County Museum of Art
Los Angeles, California

Missouri Historical Society
St. Louis, Missouri

Missouri State Park Board
Jefferson City, Missouri

Paul Moore, Jr.
Washington, D.C.
Museum of Fine Arts
Boston, Massachusetts

William Rockhill Nelson Gallery of Art
—Atkins Museum of Fine Arts
Kansas City, Missouri

The R. W. Norton Art Gallery
Shreveport, Louisiana

Peabody Museum of Archaeology
and Ethnology
Harvard University
Cambridge, Massachusetts

The Honorable Claiborne Pell
Newport, Rhode Island

James S. Rollins
Columbia, Missouri

The St. Louis Mercantile Library
Association
St. Louis, Missouri

Miss Margaret Shackelford
Washington, D.C.

Millard Watts Smith
La Jolla, California

State Historical Society of Missouri
Columbia, Missouri

Wadsworth Atheneum
Hartford, Connecticut

Washington University
St. Louis, Missouri

John Wilmerding
Hanover, New Hampshire

35. *Self-Portrait of the Artist.* circa 1877.

George Caleb Bingham: An Artist on the Frontier

The image of the frontier seen in the paintings of George Caleb Bingham came out of the artist's consciously assumed rôle as an illustrator of American western life. It was a realistic image, yet, beginning with his earliest artistic efforts, all his scenes of flatboatmen, fur traders, raftsmen, woodboatmen, and politicians were visions deliberately translated and reinterpreted by a discipline Bingham sought through self-imposed study of the works of older masters. His pictorialization of frontier life has made Bingham probably the most popular and most valued artist of our mid-nineteenth-century west. The phenomenal appearance of an artist of such stature in so isolated a place as Missouri in the early 1830s rouses art historical curiosity.

Apart from the broader considerations of style that demand a separate and more concentrated study than can be made here, it is possible to gain a rather intimate knowledge about the immediate sources of the painter in his conscious striving for sophistication and professional recognition. Within this special area, the ready availability of reproductive prints of works of art at the time was a means of self-training Bingham evidently discovered very early and one to which he continually returned throughout the forty-five years of his artistic life. Of equal importance, although

1

perhaps not experienced until slightly later in this period of self-instruction, was the contact with classical sculpture which could have come his way chiefly through collections of casts that were imported to this country in some quantity, and again by means of engraved reproductions of such works in European collections.

One can readily realize that an artist, spending his boyhood and early mature years in the heart of Missouri, far from any contact with artists, other than the self-taught or semi-schooled itinerants, would not have much opportunity to receive first-hand knowledge of the techniques and methods of the masters, nor even of relatively competent painters. Ambitious to become a painter, Bingham was compelled to seek whatever means available to develop his natural ability. As early as the age of twelve, we are told, Bingham was busily copying "such engravings as chance or friends threw his way." [1] This would have been in Franklin, a busy frontier town during the artist's childhood in the early 1820s, where there was a public library and where he could conceivably have come into contact with illustrated books. Unfortunately, none of those copies after engravings which Bingham is said to have produced at such a tender age are known.

Yet, if the reliability of the reported early contact with engravings can be trusted, Bingham had stumbled accidentally upon the means many another young painter in centuries past had used in an effort to learn from example about composition and drawing. This method of self-training was common to many of America's painters. Copley's reliance on engraved English portraits comes to mind,[2] and Dunlap informs us that both Cole and Vanderlyn relied on prints in those days when formal art training anywhere in America was almost non-existent.[3] Artist instruction books, the how-to-do-it texts of the nineteenth century, recommended this method highly, so it would also appear to have been accepted academic procedure by that time, and on an international basis as well. A typical example, chosen from a leading English drawing book, specifically recommends:

A portfolio of prints, scrupulously selected, is highly advantageous, if not absolutely necessary, as a means of acquiring valuable ideas. It is not disgraceful to the art, nor derogatory to its advanced professors, to accept the assistance of others, if they but kindle and assimilate with their own powers. The greatest caution, however, must be exercised "in the selection," and every example which is not excellent, should be rejected, as whatever is continually seen, unavoidably vitiates or improves the taste, for such is the form of habit, that where wrong impressions have once been admitted, the light of improvement may strive in vain to pierce the cloud which intercepts the rays.[4]

How a young artist on the frontier could acquire judgment in such matters is not explained by the writer of the instruction book, although the illustrations which accompany the text were chosen from the works of the great names of the distant and more recent past and could have served as a guide for his own selection.

St. Louis was described in the year of Bingham's first visit, 1835, as "the principal nursery of the fine arts in 'the far west'."[5] There he could have seen paintings, some attributed to old masters like Rubens, Veronese, and Guido Reni, and others by contemporaries like that "Parisian knight of the easel," Leon Pomarede, yet evidently he still turned to engravings as sources for his inspiration. One reporter, emerging from the young artist's St. Louis studio at that time,[6] expressed particular admiration for a copy painted by Bingham after Thomas Sully's portrait of the actress

3

Fanny Kemble which had just appeared in engraved form as an illustration in a well-known gift book annual.[7]

Either by chance or preference, the known copies executed by Bingham after engravings during his early years indicate a concentration on the works of American artists like Sully and Vanderlyn, some of which must inevitably have come his way through the then wide dissemination of the gift book with its engraved illustrations based on the paintings and designs of well-known artists of the day.[8] It is more than probable that his first acquaintanceship with the works of artists like William Sidney Mount, Daniel Huntington, and George H. Comegys, as well as other contemporaries in the East, came by means of those little volumes of literature and art which were actually being produced to help fill the growing hunger for culture then spreading rapidly across the country. It is conceivable that the visual impression made by these engraved reproductions of the works of established artists played an important part in persuading him to go to Philadelphia in 1838 where he certainly could enjoy an opportunity to see many original pictures. That, together with the possibility of obtaining formal instruction at the Pennsylvania Academy of Fine Arts, probably encouraged him to take the big step. Both of these factors seem to be implicit in his thinking at the time for he even considered making the move a permanent one, believing that there were "greater facilities" in the East.[9]

What he soon discovered, however, after a few months in the city, was that Philadelphia was almost as much a frontier town as St. Louis when it came to facilities available for formal instruction in painting. True, he was able to see and benefit by the sight of original paintings by many of his contemporaries, and certainly there was some instruction at the Academy, probably for the most part in drawing from casts after the antique, as well as lectures in anatomy, but he was no longer strictly a student and must have expected much more in the way of stimulus and opportunity. Besides, by that time, his working habits had already been formed through years of self-instruction learned at home. In a letter written to his wife just before leaving Philadelphia he clearly implies that he believed any prolonged study under the limited instruction then available there was not worthwhile:

I have been purchasing a lot of drawings and engravings, and also a lot of casts from antique sculpture which will give me nearly the same advantages in my drawing studies than are present to be enjoyed here.[10]

Considering the vast amount of reproductive prints being produced in Europe and America by the 1830s it would not have been difficult to assemble a portfolio of substantial quantity and considerable range. Line engraving in reproductive printmaking had reached its height of activity by the first decades of the nineteenth century, especially in England and on the continent. By 1830 black-and-white and color lithography had also achieved a high order of excellence which encouraged its increasing use by print publishers. Large folio prints after Hogarth and Wilkie, and older masters of painting, as well as after antique sculpture, had found their way to this country. Booksellers' lists of the period attest to this steadily growing number of prints on the market. The handsomely bound volumes of engravings after old and modern masters, such as those published by George Virtue regularly beginning in the 1840s, were another source of art reproduction. Equally noteworthy are the huge lithographic and engraved reproductions of their collections issued by European museums.

Large folio prints were also published in this country, either by freelance engravers like Asher B. Durand,[11] or by art institutions like the Apollo Association and its successor the American Art-Union, which intended them for distribution among its members. There were several excellent engravers at work in America including the indefatigable John Sartain, whose prints must have been well known to Bingham long before he had Sartain engrave reproductions of his own work. In addition to the gift books, there were other readily accessible sources, such as the illustrated magazines, which made use of engraving for embellishment.

If the visit to Philadelphia contributed little to Bingham's artistic maturity, it certainly served to make him more aware of possibilities in terms of subject matter other than portraiture. The first genre pictures of his own invention date from this period. Interestingly enough, the earliest recorded example was a subject of western connotation.[12] It follows logically that Bingham's search for study sources must have now begun to extend beyond engravings after portraits to prints of compositions involving groups of figures. With increased confidence in the value of prints for reference and study, Bingham apparently also realized the importance of classical types. He undoubtedly became familiar with the casts after the antique which formed part of the collection of the Pennsylvania Academy. They were primarily for the use of the students of the school, but were also exhibited annually along with paintings as part of the permanent holdings of the institution. In all probability, his first appreciation of the value of study from the antique models came from his contact with this collection and observation of Academy methods. Bingham's letter to his wife, quoted above, appears to bear out such an assumption. Later in life he expressed more formal views on the subject. Suggesting a purchase of casts for use by his students at the University of Missouri, he addressed himself to his friend Major Rollins in a letter written from Boonville, September 9, 1877:

A number of plaster casts from antique statuary should be found as models for pupils in Art. They are indeed indispensable, as without them the mind of the student cannot be properly imbued with those ideas of grace, elegance and truth which form the basis of genuine art. These casts are not very costly . . . .[13]

It was, in fact, a principle that Bingham lived up to all through his career, as we shall be able to observe in an analysis of a few typical examples of his work. Although none of his early drawings and studies after the antique have survived, at least one slight sketch from the Rollins scrapbook,[14] which can be dated about 1870, appears to be remotely related to the Venus de' Medici.

During the earliest years of Bingham's career, however, his main concern was with portrait painting since it was the one means of livelihood he could count on. His interest in pictorial sources would have been necessarily confined to portrait designs. Judging from the very early portraits of Dr. John Sappington and his wife, painted in 1834, as well as others which have come down to us from this period, the formula was a highly limited one. The formula of the head shown in three-quarter view, facing left, looking out toward the observer, becomes almost a trademark of the artist's style during much of the period before 1840. Bingham was obviously bound by the hard-earned lesson he certainly might have absorbed from some itinerant painter in Boonville, but it seems much more likely that he based his design on engravings he had seen, very probably after portraits by Gilbert Stuart and his circle. The metallic hardness of his contours, and even the placement of facial shadows, encourages the impression of underlying engraved sources as his primary patterns of instruction from the outset of his career.

Throughout the following years, that Bingham closely followed the instruction book's admonition in the use and particularly in the choice

of prints can be traced through the "scrupulously selected" materials that increasingly attracted his attention and influenced his further efforts. His noteworthy admiration for Thomas Sully can be followed from the copy he reportedly made after the engraved portrait of Fanny Kemble, painted in 1835, to the stylistic influence visible in the portraits he produced during the 1840s after he had obviously had ample opportunity to see original works by the artist. As late as 1877 Bingham still turned on occasion to Sully for inspiration, at that time very probably adopting the motif for his *Palm Leaf Shade* (Figure 1) from a similar portrait by Sully which had appeared in a gift annual many years earlier (Figure 2).[15]

Sully's influence is evident, too, in at least one of Bingham's earlier genre compositions, *The Mill Boy*, actually one section of a two-sided

Figure 1, facing page, left
Bingham, *Palm Leaf Shade*, 1877/78
Coll: Mrs. Kathleen T. Stier, Lexington, Missouri

Figure 2, facing page, right
Lady with Fan, engraving by J. Cheney after Thomas Sully

Figure 3, right
Thomas Sully, *The Torn Hat*, 1820
Coll: Museum of Fine Arts, Boston

processional banner which the artist was commissioned to prepare in connection with the presidential campaign held in Boonville in the fall of 1844. Since this was one of the first commissions of any importance received by Bingham since his return to Missouri after an absence of four years in Washington, he very probably also sought to make good use of this opportunity to draw attention to his newly acquired ability in a field beyond portraiture. Significantly, then it was the Sullyesque sophistication he wished to emulate and demonstrate on this occasion. The head of *The Mill Boy*, painted in the idealized portrait style of the master, closely resembles the boy in *The Torn Hat* (Figure 3), a painting he could have seen but which was also available through a gift-book engraving published in 1829.[16]

From Sully, the "American Lawrence," to Sir Thomas Lawrence himself was but one step removed, and a step Bingham obviously took very soon in his portrait-painting career. Although it is doubtful that the artist ever had an occasion to see an original work by the English master during his early Missouri years, he was evidently familiar with reproductions made after his more important portraits. There are several instances of such contact, but the most obvious and possibly the most fascinating example is his adaptation of Lawrence's painting *Miss Emily Anderson as Little Red Hood* (Figure 4). The picture was probably known to Bingham and his contemporaries only in reproduction, most likely through its appearance in gift-books.[17] He seems to have been already familiar with the composition in 1837 when he painted one of his earliest full-length portraits, that of a child of the Rollins family, adopting the general pose but none of the story connotation (the vogue for "Little Red Riding Hood" does not gain much headway in America before 1845 but grows steadily from the 1850s on). In one of his last portraits, *Miss Eulalie Hockaday as Little Red Riding Hood* (Figure 5), by coincidence also that of a Rollins child, both pose and motif are taken over although sufficiently altered to suit the taste of the time by heightening the narrative element (the wolf) and by bringing the child's costume up to date.

Portraits of Bingham's middle and late years reflect his growing freedom from artistic limitations through the use of a greater variety of pictorial sources than ever before. This becomes particularly evident as important public and private commissions come his way. Thus, in searching out these sources, it is no more surprising to discover that a seventeenth-century etching of one of the Seasons served him as a probable basis for the portrait of a Boonville matron than it is to find the portrait of an Indian chief translated into that of a St. Louis settler. Official portraits were most coveted by artists although they offered little opportunity for

Figure 4. Miss Emily Anderson as Little Red Riding Hood,
engraving by J. Sartain after Sir Thomas Lawrence

Figure 5. Bingham, *Miss Eulalie Hockaday as Little Red Riding Hood*, 1878/79
Coll: Mrs. E. H. Bartlett, Kansas City, Missouri

unusual or dramatic effects due to the stringent requirements usually set by the conservative committees appointed to approve such commissions. Bingham may have been already aware of the problem when he painted the small full–length portrait *John Cumming Edwards* in 1844 in which he attempted to introduce an original note in an otherwise formal composition. Whether the portrait was intended as a model or a demonstration piece to encourage an official order is not known. But we can assume that Bingham pondered the pictorial problem and sought a new solution

11

through the example of others. In this instance, the resemblance to Samuel F. B. Morse's portrait *Marquis de Lafayette* (City of New York, 1825–1826), still considered one of the finest official portraits produced by an American artist, can be no mere coincidence. Bingham could have had contact with the painting for his primary inspiration and then sought out reproduction for further reference and study.

A brief examination of a few of Bingham's genre subjects of the period beginning about 1845 reveals the free and varied use the artist learned to make of the pictorial and three-dimensional sources which came his way. It is important to note that Bingham rarely, if ever, made direct, copies of the works of other artists during these and succeeding years.[18] He was selective in his use of the sources within his reach in developing the narrative compositions which have earned him so respected a place among American artists. Apart from those broad elements of compositional design undoubtedly digested from instruction books, single figures and groups of figures, as well as background ideas, were almost always studied and translated from a variety of art historical sources.

The relationship between Bingham's first *The Jolly Flatboatmen* (1846) (Figure 6) and Sir David Wilkie's *Blind Fiddler* (Figure 7) is by no means remote. The Scottish master was one of the most popular genre painters of the day, admired both in his own country and abroad, although it seems unlikely that his works were known in America other than from engraved reproductions. William Sidney Mount, whose manner is reminiscent of Wilkie, and who must also have been thoroughly acquainted with the master's work through engravings, was recognized in his time as the "American Wilkie." Those parallels which can be drawn between Bingham and Mount, indicating Bingham's lively awareness of the work of the Long Island painter, actually reflect more a shared inspiration and a

Figure 6
Bingham, *The Jolly Flatboatmen* (1), 1846
Coll: The Hon. Claiborne Pell, Newport, Rhode Island

Figure 8
Bingham, *The Jolly Flatboatmen* (2), ca. 1848
Coll: Mastin Kratz, Kansas City, Missouri

Figure 7
The Blind Fiddler, engraving by C. W. Sharpe after Sir David
Wilkie (Hall, S.C. *Gems of European Art*, 1846)

Figure 9
Dancing Faun from Casa del Fauno, Pompeii
Coll: Museo Nazionale, Naples

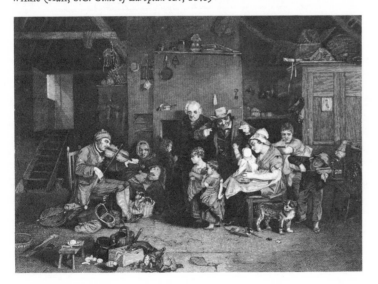

probable common source in Wilkie. For *The Jolly Flatboatmen* Bingham took over the figure motifs of the fiddler tapping his foot to keep time and the central figure snapping his fingers. In some engravings, the design is actually reversed so that the figures appear in positions similar to Bingham's composition, but this is not necessarily of significance in this consideration. Much more to the point is the fact that by the time Bingham composed this picture he had moved far beyond the mere copying from prints and had learned to extract and freely adapt only those ideas which he needed for his own pictures—a practice followed by the old masters of past centuries. Although the instruction books broadly suggested this method, both in text and illustration, it is still a matter of no small wonder that an artist on the American frontier could arrive independently at a means of working recognized as standard procedure by generations of his European predecessors.

The growing maturity of the artist is further evidenced in his second *The Jolly Flatboatmen* (circa 1848) (Figure 8). In an obvious attempt to avoid a repetition of the strict frontality and frozen movement of the first version, he eliminated the central figure of the dancer snapping his fingers, replacing it with the graceful figure of a dancer whose open silhouette provided precisely the variety he desired in the revised composition. And, in a manner consistent with Bingham's procedure in succeeding years, the pose of the new motif can be identified as derived ultimately from the familiar Hellenistic figure *Dancing Faun* (Figure 9).

The same dancing figure appears in the third and largest of Bingham's flatboatmen series, *Jolly Flatboatmen in Port*, which he painted in Düsseldorf. This elaborate painting reflects the artist's continuing interest in large-scale, multi-figured compositions and there can be little doubt that he also continued his usual method, during the course of this major work, in seeking out solutions to problems of a similar nature made by other masters. Despite his admiration for the Düsseldorfian School and its teaching methods, Bingham did not come to Germany as a student. What he observed there did have its ultimate effect on his technical method but more importantly there is little evidence of his concern with contemporary German pictorial ideas. It seems particularly evident in this flatboatmen subject which, despite its Düsseldorfian high finish, may very possibly owe more to Géricault's *The Raft of the Medusa* (1818–1819) than to any other comparable composition. The mood is quite different, of course, but the monumental pyramid of classically inspired figures on a raft, its apex reached by the signaling figure, would certainly have held Bingham's attention down to the last detail. Géricault's painting had actually appeared in American publications by this time,[19] and had been otherwise reproduced, although the picture may also have been on view when Bingham arrived in Paris in 1856.

For another of his western subjects, the *Raftsmen Playing Cards* (1847), and a second version called *In a Quandary* (1851) (Figure 10), Bingham had available many engravings after paintings in which the card player occurs as a central subject, which could have afforded inspiration for his own version. The same subject by Wilkie could have suggested a mood at least. But it was almost certainly a composition by Louis-Léopold Boilly (Figure 11), lithographed in 1825, that offered him a more positive inspiration. The relationship in the poses of the two card players and the manner in which the cards are held and displayed in the two pictures seem more than coincidental.

One of the artist's rare historical subjects, *The Emigration of Daniel Boone* (1851) (Figure 12), reveals yet another interesting combination of models taken from sources already well established in his repertoire.

The general scheme of composition, a central group of figures flanked on either side by wild foliage, appears to have been suggested by a mezzotint by Sartain after a painting by Peter F. Rothermel (Figure 13) which had appeared in a gift book two years before Bingham began his picture.[20] The Rothermel version concerned itself with a similar theme, and was called *The Pioneers*.

Bingham always made careful preliminary drawing studies for individual figures. His strong admiration for classical models is again visible in the poses of two of the pioneers. Daniel Boone strides forward like the Doryphorus (Figure 14), with only the position of the legs reversed, while the figure at his left ties his moccasin in the manner of his ancestor the *Jason* or *Cincinnatus* (Figure 15).

Without doubt the most ambitious pictures of Bingham's career as a painter of western genre were his series on election subjects. He lavished

Figure 10, left
Bingham, *In a Quandary* or *Mississippi Raftmen at Cards*, 1851
Coll: Paul Moore, Jr., Washington, D.C.

Figure 11, below
The Card Players, lithograph after Louis-Loépold Boilly, 1825

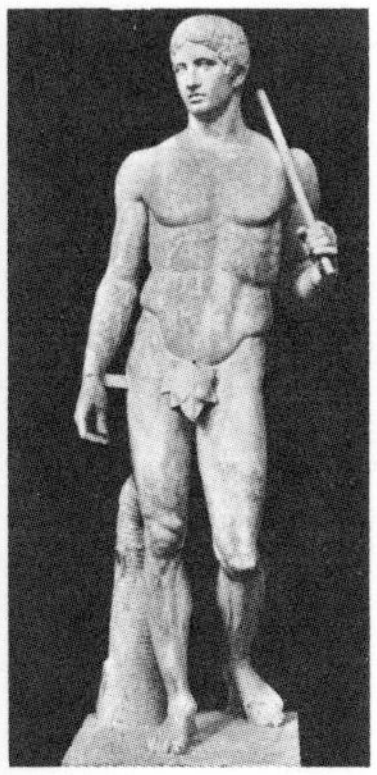

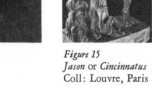

Figure 14
Doryphorus (Spearbearer)
Coll: Museo Nazionale, Naples

Figure 12
Bingham, *The Emigration of Daniel Boone*, 1851
Coll: Washington University, St. Louis, Missouri

Figure 15
Jason or *Cincinnatus*
Coll: Louvre, Paris

Figure 13
The Pioneers, engraving by J. Sartain
after Peter F. Rothermel

on these all the knowledge and experience he had gained in his self-directed studies. In the series, *The County Election* (1851–1852) (Figure 16) is of particular interest in this connection.

Following his usual practice, the artist must have sought out compositions involving many figures for preliminary study. William Hogarth's election pictures were widely known in Bingham's time through engravings published after the paintings. It seems entirely logical to discover them to have been the obvious primary sources for *The County Election*. As in the case of *The Emigration of Daniel Boone*, the similarity of the theme itself is too striking to be mere coincidence. That *The County Election* took its general form and plan from Hogarth's *Canvassing for Votes* (Figure 17), was recognized some time ago.[21] Bingham evidently based his composition on an engraving in reverse of the original painting. He used the main elements of the large architectural screen at the right, with its diminishing line of buildings but substituted characteristic buildings and countryside which described the local Missouri scene for Hogarth's typically English background. The balancing smaller wing at the left was also adopted from Hogarth although with some modification. The motif of the refreshment stand and the drinker is common to both pictures, and there is a decided similarity between the group of figures at the center of the Hogarth composition and the conversation group standing beneath the portico at the right in *The County Election*. Yet apart from those elements of design and motif, and possible inspiration of the subject itself, Bingham followed his own line of genial anecdote on a typical western election scene. Hogarth's special brand of biting satire was entirely foreign to Bingham's temperament and purpose.

Derivation from classical models appears in at least one figure, that of the boy in the left foreground, playing mumble-the-peg. Since the artist's

Figure 16
Bingham, *The County Election* (1), 1851/52
Coll: City Art Museum of St. Louis, St. Louis, Missouri

Figure 17
Canvassing for Votes, engraving after William Hogarth, 1758

Figure 19
The Writing Masters engraving by H. Wallis after Frans van Meiris (Hall, S.C. "Gems of European Art," 1846)

pattern is now a familiar one, it comes as no surprise to discover that the figure closely resembles the pose of a statue in the collections of the British Museum which could have been known to Bingham through an engraving (Figure 18). And need one wonder greatly at the close resemblance between the clerk shaping his quill, at the upper right, and the subject of an engraving (Figure 19) based on a painting by Frans van Meiris?

But Bingham's continual search for pictorial source materials did not concern itself specifically with motif and detail. For the most part his greatest concern was with the larger aspects of compositional design, and particularly with the problem of giving pictorial unity and meaning to those pictures of many pictures that occupied most of his attention during the 1850s. In such instances it seems fairly obvious that he followed the directions of the instruction books in which appeared outline drawings based on the works of the masters intended to concentrate the student's attention to mass and structure rather than to distracting detail. One can perhaps come closest to Bingham's reliance on such procedure in comparing the two versions of *The Verdict of the People* (the first in the Boatmen's National Bank of St. Louis, the second in the collection of The R. W. Norton Art Gallery, Shreveport, La.). The essential differences between the two pictures are in the basic compositional orgnization of light and dark masses in which the artist strives for a variety of effects all aimed at a unity of form and content. His procedure, which can be effectively demonstrated here, was to make use of the diagrammatic references supplied by the instruction book (in this case Samuel Prout) [22] and then to refer to reproductions of the works of masters in which such methods were used with good results, at the same time also selecting details. At this point, for example, Bingham might have had reference to Wilkie's *Chelsea Pensioners Reading the Gazette of the Battle of Waterloo*, which shares several characteristics in common with Bingham's composition. And the classical note may also be seen in comparing Bingham s figure of the drunken man seated on the ground in the foregound with the Hellenistic figure of the so-called *Dying Gaul*.

Through the mid-1850s Bingham still turned to Wilkie's pictures for his first thoughts in developing a new theme. The always cheerful, smiling, and at times musical mood, so consistently present in the English master's subjects, must have struck a sympathetic note that Bingham sought to achieve and maintain in his own work. He was successful in this effort to a large extent, although he was almost always able to lend a somewhat greater strength to his own pictures through a more dominant personal note of descriptive realism that was alien to Wilkie's nature and envionment. A good example can be given by making a comparison of Bingham's *Woodboatmen on a River* (Figure 20) with Wilkie's painting known as *The Jew's Harp* (Figure 21). It seems entirely probable that he

Figure 20, left
Bingham, *Woodboatmen on a River*, 1854
Coll: Museum of Fine Arts, Boston, Massachusetts

Figure 21, above
The Jew's Harp, engraving by E. Smith after Sir David Wilkie (Hall, S.C. "Gems of European Art," 1846)

derived his initial inspiration from the Wilkie composition. In both pictures the rather unusual motif of the jew's harp player serves to set a mood and certainly forms the main subject concentration, although Bingham's descriptive note is several shades removed from the obviously more sentimental interpretation found in Wilkie

Although Bingham possibly was acquainted with prints taken from paintings by artists of the Düsseldorf school, their direct or indirect formal influence on the painter cannot be discerned until his sojourn in that city from 1856 to 1859. This period postdates his major efforts in genre and is well after the crest of their popularity had been reached. Yet during the Düsseldorf stay, and in the years that followed before he finally laid down his brush in the summer of 1879, Bingham never departed from his established use of those source materials which had long since become his *modus operandi*. What happened to the artist at Düsseldorf was a distinct loss of the painterly style he had attained by the mid 1850s through long and persistent effort based preeminently on a conscious self-criticism.

The first large subject he undertook in the years following his return from Germany was *Order No. 11* (1865-circa 1868) (Figure 22). The subject, taken from then recent history, is typical of the dramatic style favored by the men of Düsseldorf, as is the tight drawing and hard finish that Bingham unfortunately sought to emulate on this occasion. But beyond that, the painting forms a most effective example with which to conclude this brief investigation of the various sources used by the artist. The picture represents perhaps the artist's greatest mélange of motifs drawn from sources of the past up to that time, although they were infused with a spirit quite different from the originals. From this painting it can be safely assumed that Bingham had considerably enlarged his portfolio of prints, and hence his range of sources, during the three-year stay abroad.

Figure 22, below, left
Bingham, *Martial Law* or *Order No. 11* (2), ca. 1869/70
Coll: State Historical Society of Missouri, Columbia, Missouri

Figure 26, below, right
Masaccio, *The Expulsion*
Brancacci Chapel, S. Maria del Carmine, Florence

Figure 24,
Apollo Belvedere
Coll: Vatican, Rome

Figure 25,
Fra Bartolommeo, *Pieta*
Coll: Pitti Palace, Florence

Figure 23,
Jean-Baptiste Greuze, *The Father's Curse*
Coll: Louvre, Paris

The central group, consisting of an old man, and the girl and child who cling to him, seems to have been freely adapted from Jean-Baptiste Greuze's composition, *The Father's Curse* (Figure 23). The violent gesture of the man, so important for the Greuze design, was considerably changed, however, to better satisfy Bingham's artistic aims. Striving, as always, to incorporate into his pictures those elements of classical art which he firmly believed formed "the basis of genuine art," he substituted a figure which must have been derived ultimately from the *Apollo Belvedere* (Figure 24).

The fainting woman supported by a Negro servant, as well as the woman bending over her fallen husband, recall the central figures of a *Pietà* by Fra Bartolommeo (Figure 25). And the weeping Negro walking off at the far right appears to be a distant relative of Masaccio's Adam from the *Expulsion* in the Brancacci Chapel of the church of Santa Maria del Carmine in Florence (Figure 26).

Thus did classical antiquity, the Italian fifteenth and sixteenth, and the French eighteenth centuries all play a significant role in a Düsseldorfian drama staged on the Kansas-Missouri frontier in the mid-1860s.

During the final decade of his life Bingham seriously considered newspaper illustration as a logical outlet for his dormant talent.[23] He apparently received little encouragement to paint story-telling pictures. We thus have only an occasional glimpse of his artistic thinking at the time. The one or two genre pictures he produced during these years reflect at least in subject the style which earned him fame earlier. Another clue is revealed in a copy he made about 1877 after a reproduction of Sir Edwin Landseer's *Spaniels of King Charles' Breed* (Bingham's copy is known as *Guarding Their Master's Hat*) and in the self-portrait he painted about the same time which also apparently was inspired by Landseer's portrait of himself, *The Connoisseurs*, and certainly known to Bingham through reproduction. From our vantage point Bingham was, as in the past, still trying to keep abreast of contemporary fashion in painting and still making good use of available pictorial sources.

In landscape Bingham adopted much the same procedure he followed in his other artistic endeavors. Landscapes first occur as background in several of the portraits he painted before 1840 and it can also be assumed that he painted pure landscapes by that time. Among extant pictures, however, only *Cottage Scenery* gives us an idea of the artist's early style. Bingham's source, both in general scheme and in detail, is obviously the English landscapist George Morland, whose works he could scarcely have seen in the original at this time. He would have come closest to the style through the landscapes of Joshua Shaw in Philadelphia, but for the groupings of rustic details he would still have had to refer to the reproductions of Morland's pictures and to the pattern books of his motifs which were then readily available in publication.

Most of Bingham's landscapes of the latter 1840s and early 1850s, such as *Landscape with Cattle* (City Art Museum of St. Louis, 1846) and the various landscapes with deer and fishermen are "fancy pictures" with no particular reference to place. They are chiefly skillfully composed arrangements of trees and groups of cattle or other motifs which are the results of studio studies taken from instruction-book models, pattern-books, and engravings after the works of well-known landscape painters. In *The Storm* Bingham seems to have been inspired by the imaginative landscapes of Thomas Cole and, in a quieter mood, such as in *Landscape with Deer* by the more conservative manner of Asher Brown Durand or

Thomas Doughty. In *Landscape: Mountain View* the panoramic impulse already foreshadows the kind of landscape school which was later dominated by Albert Bierstadt. And by the 1870s, when huge descriptive paintings were all the rage, Bingham painted his first *View of Pike's Peak* (1872, now lost), making use of a number of preparatory studies made on the spot but which, in general scheme, owes much to Frederic E. Church's *Heart of the Andes*, a painting he could have known both in the original and in reproduction.

During the course of his career as a landscape painter Bingham clearly ran the full gamut of expression, keeping ever aware of the changing taste of the time. Yet all of his sources, whether seen or learned through reproduction, reveal a conscious selection from models of classical design which seem never to allow nature's whim to dominate the artist's sense of academic order.

I believe that we may safely estimate, on the basis of the few examples just discussed, that Bingham's selection of his pictorial source materials was not necessarily conditioned by any historical preference. It is obvious that he was well aware of contemporary artistic taste in evolving his own style and it can also be considered no mere coincidence that the names of established contemporaries like Sully and Wilkie turn up so frequently. Generally speaking, however, Bingham regarded himself as completely free to move in any direction he chose in assembling available study and source materials although, as the instruction book had long since advised, the selection was unquestionably "scrupulously" made on the basis of his particular concern with ideas of composition, theme, and specific motif. That he would often refer to classical models was inevitable as he strained to bring to his work the respectability of academic art. Whether he ever achieved the sophistication in the grand manner he so desired seems scarcely of any real significance in estimating his achievement. What does seem important is the fact that Bingham, like many another artist on the frontier, discovered through self-training and using secondary sources, an artistic direction that was actually not out of step with that taken by many of his European contemporaries who had much more favorable opportunities available for study. The works of an artist like George Caleb Bingham are therefore all the more remarkable if only considered in terms of what could indeed take place on the American frontier.

E. Maurice Bloch

275-849 O—67——3

Notes

1. *Bulletin of the American Art-Union*, vol. II (August 1849), p. 11.

2. Flexner, J. T., *American Paintings: First Flowers of Our Wilderness*, Boston, 1947, pp. 217–[219].

3. Dunlap, W., *History of the Rise and Progress of the Arts of Design in the United States*, New York, 1834, vol. II, pp. 32, 352.

4. Prout, S., *Hints on Light and Shade . . .*, London, 1848, p. B.2(3). First published in London in 1838; appeared in booksellers list (Carey & Hart, Philadelphia), in 1839.

5. *Missouri Intelligencer* (Columbia), March 14, 1835, 3–1.

6. *Jeffersonian Republican* (Jefferson City), January 2, 1836, 4–2 (from *St. Louis Bulletin*).

7. *The Gift: A Christmas and New Year's Present for 1836*, Phildelphia, [1835], frontispiece.

8. Gift book annuals of the period actually show a preponderant interest in American art. A systematic survey of two representative annuals revealed that 119 of 230 identified engraved illustrations used were after paintings and designs by American artists. (Lovejoy, D. S., "American Painting in Early Nineteenth Century Gift Books," *American Quarterly*, vol. VII [1955], p. 346).

9. Letter, Bingham to J. S. Rollins, Natchez, Mississippi, May 6, 1837, (*Missouri Historical Review*, vol. XXXII [1937], p. 7).

10. Letter, Phildelphia, June 3, 1838, coll. State Historical Society of Missouri, Columbia, Missouri.

11. Bingham reportedly made a copy of Vanderlyn's *Ariadne*, based on Durand's well-known engraving. (*National Intelligencer*, [Washington,

D.C.] February 17, 1841, quoted by McDermott, J. F., *George Caleb Bingham, River Portraitist*, Norman, Oklahoma, 1959, p. 37).

12. *Western Boatmen Ashore.* Exhibited at the Apollo Gallery, New York City, fall, 1838.

13. *Missouri Historical Review*, vol. XXXIII (1939), pp. 381–382.

14. Coll. State Historical Society of Missouri, Columbia, Missouri.

15. *The Gift: A Christmas and New Year's Present for 1839*, Philadelphia, [1838], title vignette.

16. *Youth's Keepsake, a Christmas and New Year's Gift for Young People*, Boston, Carter & Hendee, 1830. Engraved by John Cheney.

17. *The Atlantic Souvenir . . .*, Philadelphia, Carey & Lea, 1828, opp. p. 97 (Engraved by J. B. Longacre); *The Wild Flower: a Gift Book for the Holydays*, for 1852, Philadelphia, 1852, opp. p. 103.

18. As late as 1870, however, brief pencil sketches by Bingham occur in the Rollins scrapbook which reveal at least a memory of such pictures as Titian's *Danaë* and *Lavinia*.

19. *Illustrated Magazine of Art*, (New York), vol. II (1853), 284; lithographed by Géricault and Charlet, circa 1820 and by Charles E. Motte to illustrate Alexandre Correard's *Naufrage de la Frégate La Meduse*, published circa 1821; also engraved by Alphonse A. Leroy, probably by 1847.

20. *The Opal, A Pure Gift for All Seasons*, New York, 1849, opp. p. 143.

21. [Newman, H. S.], "Accident of Design? Bingham's County Election and Hogarth's Canvassing for Votes," *Antiques*, vol. XXXVII (1940), pp. 92–93.

22. Prout, *op. cit.*, Pl. XV (3).

23. Letter, Bingham to J. S. Rollins, Kansas City, October 26, 1873 (*Missouri Historical Review*, vol. XXXIII [1939], p. 349.)

Catalog of the Exhibition

This information on the works included in the present exhibition was compiled by Dr. E. Maurice Bloch and is based on his research. Dr. Bloch's notes on the works are identified by his initials.

Dimensions are in inches; height x width. Works reproduced are marked*.

PAINTINGS

1. *Dr. John Sappington* 1776–1856   1834

   Oil on canvas: 27 x 21¾. Inscribed near center, right: "Aged 59./ 1834."

   Probably painted at subject's residence, "Fox Castle," near Arrow Rock, Saline County, Missouri. As late as 1944, ownership was claimed by Mrs. Eramus Darwin Sappington II (Mamie Miller) (letter, C. Lester Hall, Jr., to E. Maurice Bloch, June 10, 1944).

EXHIBITION: Kansas City, Missouri, William Rockhill Nelson Gallery of Art, 1953 (no. 114).

REFERENCE: McDermott, pp. 20, 179, 422 (no. 5), ill. Pl. 1.

Subject, a pioneer Missouri physician, was born May 15, 1776, in Maryland; died September 7, 1856, Arrow Rock, Missouri. The son of Dr. Mark Brown and Rebecca (Boyce) Sappington, he spent his youth with his family in Nashville, Tennessee, studying medicine with his father, but later moved to Franklin, Tennessee, to practice alone. He married Jane Breathitt, sister of Governor John Breathitt of Kentucky, November 22, 1804. In 1817 he resided in Howard County, Missouri, later moving to Saline County, establishing his permanent residence there, near Arrow Rock. He did much to revolutionize pioneer medical practice in Missouri and in other regions afflicted with malaria, a disease so prevalent at the time that it was one of the greatest obstacles with which the settlers had to contend. Soon after quinine became available in this country, Sappington recognized its specific nature in the treatment of malaria and advocated its use without recourse to older, more violent methods. Recognizing the urgent need of making quinine available, he began, in 1832, the wholesale distribution of Dr. Sappington's Anti-Fever Pills. He also wrote and published his *Theory and Treatment of Fevers*, issued at Arrow Rock in 1842, perhaps the first medical treatise written and published west of the Mississippi. (*Dictionary of American Biography* [hereafter cited as *D.A.B.*], XVI, p. 353; MSS, C. Lester Hall, Jr.)

Lent by the Missouri State Park Board

2. *Mrs. John Sappington* (Jane Breathitt) 1783–1852   1834

Oil on canvas: 27 x 21¾. Inscribed near center, right: "Aged 51./1834."

Probably painted at the subject's residence, "Fox Castle," near Arrow Rock, Saline County, Missouri. As late as 1944, ownership was claimed by Mrs. Eramus Darwin Sappington II (Mamie Miller). (Letter, C. Lester Hall, Jr., to E. Maurice Bloch, June 10, 1944).

EXHIBITION: Kansas City, Missouri, William Rockhill Nelson Gallery of Art, 1953 (no. 115)

REFERENCES: R. E. Taggart, " 'Canvassing for a Vote' and Some Unpublished Portraits by Bingham," *Art Quarterly*, XVIII (1955), pp. 232, 235, illus. Fig. 2; McDermott, pp. 20, 175–176, 179, 422 (no. 5), illus. Pl. 2.

SUBJECT was born in Henry County, Virginia, October 13, 1783, the eldest child of William and Elizabeth (Whittsett) Breathitt; died November 14, 1852, in Saline County, Missouri. She married Dr. John Sappington, November 22, 1804, residing with her husband first in Howard County, Missouri, in 1819, and later in Saline County, near Arrow Rock. The mother of nine children; one daughter was married to Governor Meredith Miles Marmaduke of Missouri; three others, in succession, to Governor Claiborne Fox Jackson of Missouri. She was also the sister of Governor John Breathitt of Kentucky. (Letter, C. Lester Hall, Jr., to E. Maurice Bloch, March 2, 1945.)

Lent by the Missouri State Park Board

3. *Thomas Miller* 1811–1841   1837

    Oil on canvasboard: 3½ x 2½ (oval)

    Probably painted at Columbia, Missouri; owned by Major James Sidney Rollins; inherited by his son, Curtis Burnam Rollins; presented to his daughter, Mrs. W. D. A. Westfall (Ruth Rollins), before 1917; all of Columbia, Missouri; transferred to present owner, 1961.

REFERENCES: Rusk, pp. 24, 119, ill. Pl. XIII; *Missouri Historical Review* [hereafter cited as *M.H.R.*], XXXII (1937), p. 8, n. 4 (C.B.R.); Christ-Janer, p. 27; *M.H.R.*, LVI (1962), pp. 115, 136; McDermott, pp. 26, 424 (no. 37).

SUBJECT was born in Hopewell Township, Washington County, Pennsylvania, March 7, 1811; died en route to Santa Fe, New Mexico, September 15, 1841. Educated at Washington College (now Washington and Jefferson University) in Washington, Pennsylvania, and at Indiana University, where he graduated in 1831. He went to Transylvania University Law School in Lexington, Kentucky, graduating in 1833, and afterward held a teaching post there. When Columbia College (later the University of Missouri) was established, he was named its first president in 1834, an appointment that is said to have been made chiefly on the recommendation of his friend and former classmate James Sidney Rollins. He resigned the post in 1836 to practice law, becoming a partner of Rollins at Columbia, Missouri. The two men also acquired a newspaper, *The Missouri Intelligencer and Boon's Lick Advertiser*, changing its name to *The Columbia Patriot*. (*M.H.R.*, XXXII [1937], p. 8, n. 4; R. R. Westfall, "Thomas Miller," *M.H.R.*, LVI [1962], pp. 136–145).

Lent by the State Historical Society of Missouri

4. *Mrs. Thomas Shackelford* (Eliza Chives Pulliam), 1779–1851   1838–1839

Oil on canvas: 35½ x 29½. Inscribed on card held by subject: "To my children/When deprived of my counsel, forget not my precepts, Shun vice, love virtue./January 1, 1839."

"Painted in Saline County, Missouri, at the old Shackelford home about two miles north of the little town of Gilliam" (letter, Mrs. G. C. Shackelford to E. Maurice Bloch, June 26, 1944). Said to have been commissioned by son, Judge Thomas Shackelford (1822–1908), of Glasgow, Missouri; inherited by his son, George Carlisle Shackelford (b. 1877), of Kansas City, Missouri; to his wife; to their daughters, the present owners.

EXHIBITION: Kansas City, Missouri, William Rockhill Nelson Gallery of Art, 1953 (no. 116).

REFERENCES: Rusk, pp. 26, 119; R. E. Taggart, "'Canvassing for a Vote and Some Unpublished Portraits by Bingham,'' *Art Quarterly*, XVIII (1955), pp. 235–236, illus. Fig. 6; McDermott, pp. 23, 31, 33, 177, 179, 424 (no. 48), illus. Pl. 12.

SUBJECT was born in Tennessee and married in Nashville in 1817, becoming the second wife of Thomas Shackelford (1776–1835). She had two daughters by the time the family left Nashville for Missouri in 1819. They settled in Saline County, eventually acquiring a large farm near the present town of Gilliam. She died there March 9, 1851.

Lent by Miss Margaret Shackelford

5. *Judge Henry Lewis* 1782–1873   1839

    Oil on canvas: 29 x 22

    Painted near Glasgow, Missouri; owned by subject and inherited by his family; John Lewis; Mrs. Emma L. Lewis, Fayette, Missouri; Mrs. James Watts; to her son Millard F. Watts; to his daughter, Mrs. Richard Hawes (Laura May Watts Smith), St. Louis, Missouri.: to her son, the present owner.

REFERENCES: Rusk, p. 119; McDermott, pp. 26, 424 (no. 32).

E.M.B. Dated 1837 by Rusk on basis of "information obtained from relatives and friends of the persons represented." Stylistically, however, it belongs to the later date.

SUBJECT was born in Buckingham County, Virginia, November 14, 1782; died Glasgow, Missouri, June 22, 1873.

Lent by Millard Watts Smith

6. *Mrs. Henry Lewis* (Elizabeth Morton Woodson) 1790–1857   1839

    Oil on canvas: 29 x 22

    Painted near Glasgow, Missouri; owned by subject and husband; inherited by family; John Lewis; Mrs. Emma L. Lewis, Fayette,

Missouri; Mrs. James Watts; to her son Millard F. Watts; to his daughter, Mrs. Richard Hawes (Laura May Watts Smith), St. Louis, Missouri; to her son, the present owner.

REFERENCES: Rusk, p. 119; McDermott, pp. 26, 424 (no. 33).

E.M.B. Dated 1837 by Rusk on basis of "information obtained from relatives and friends of the persons represented." Stylistically, however, it belongs to the later date.

SUBJECT was born in Prince Edward County, Virginia, April 22, 1790, the daughter of Jacob and Elizabeth (Morton) Woodson. She was married there to Henry Lewis. They moved with her father's family to Missouri in 1817, settling on a farm near Glasgow, Howard County. (H. M. Woodson, *Historical Genealogy of the Woodsons and Their Connections*, p. 94.) She died in Glasgow, September 28, 1857.

Lent by Millard Watts Smith

7. *Mrs. George Caleb Bingham* (Sarah Elizabeth Hutchison)
   1819–1848 *and Son Newton* 1837–1841   1840–1841

   Oil on canvas: 35 x 29

   Painted in Washington, District of Columbia; in possession of the artist; inherited by his daughter, Mrs. Thomas Benton King (Clara Bingham, 1845–1900), and her husband, Stephenville, Texas; to their daughter, present owner.

REFERENCES: Rusk, p. 120; McDermott, p. 426 (no. 69).

SUBJECT, Sara Elizabeth Hutchison Bingham, was the first wife of the artist, born 1819, the daughter of Nathaniel Hutchison; died Arrow Rock, Missouri, November 29, 1848. She married George Caleb Bingham in Boonville, Missouri, April, 1836.

SUBJECT, Newton Bingham, the eldest son of the artist and his first wife, was born in Natchez, Mississippi, March 26, 1837, and died Washington, District of Columbia, March 13, 1841.

Lent by Mrs. William Perrin Bowdry

8. *John Quincy Adams* 1767–1848   1844

   Oil on panel: 10 x 7¾

   Probably painted from life at Washington, District of Columbia; undoubtedly acquired by Major James Sidney Rollins from the artist; inherited by his son, George Bingham Rollins, later part of his estate; to his daughter, Mrs. John D. Von Holtzendorff (Margaret Rollins); to present owner; all of Columbia, Missouri.

Exhibition: Columbia, Missouri, University of Missouri, 1910 (no. 23).

Document: John Quincy Adams noted six sittings to Bingham in his diary for the month of May 1844 which are believed to refer to this portrait. (MSS coll. Massachusetts Historical Society, Boston, Mass.; C. F. Adams, ed., *Memoirs of John Quincy Adams*, vol. 12, pp. 32, 35.)

References: Rusk, pp. 29–30, 120, ill. Pl. XVI; Christ-Janer, p. 33; McDermott, pp. 43–44, 426 (no. 83); Bolton, Theodore *Early American Portrait Painters in Miniature*, New York, F. F. Sherman, 1921, p. 10 (no. 1).

E.M.B. A later copy by Bingham of this portrait, with slight variation, is now in the collection of The Detroit Institute of Arts.

Subject was the sixth President of the United States, 1824–1828, born July 11, 1767, Braintree (now Quincy), Massachusetts; died Feb. 23, 1848, Washington, District of Columbia. The eldest son of John and Abigail (Smith) Adams. Married Louisa Catherine Johnson, July 26, 1797. He was commissioned minister to the Netherlands by George

Washington in 1794, and afterward served other diplomatic missions abroad. At a later date he was minister to Russia, 1809; minister to England, 1815–1817. Elected to Senate in 1803; resigned in 1808. He was secretary of state under Monroe in 1817. After serving his office as President, Adams was returned to Congress as a representative in 1831, a post he held until his death. (*D.A.B.*, I, pp. 84–92.)

Lent by James S. Rollins

9. *The Mill Boy: The Boonville Juvenile Clay Club Banner*   1844

Oil on canvas: 37¼ x 46½

Painted at Boonville, Missouri, between mid-September and October 10, 1844. Commissioned by the Boonville Juvenile Clay Club and borne in procession during the Whig convention held in the town in connection with the presidential election, October 10, 1844; in the possession of Miss Haden, Boonville, Missouri, 1945; inherited by Mrs. Leslie Cowan.

EXHIBITIONS: Kansas City, Missouri, William Rockhill Nelson Gallery of Art, 1961 (no. 3A); St. Louis, Missouri, City Art Museum of St. Louis, 1961 (no. 3A).

REFERENCES: *Boonville* (Missouri) *Observer*, October 15, 1844, 2–1; E. M. Bloch, "Art in Politics," *Art in America*, XXXII (1945), pp. 93–100, illus. opp. p. 99; McDermott, pp. 48, 48 n., 413 (nos. 22, 23), illus. Pl. 17.

E.M.B. The banner was probably painted in two sections, mounted and carried back to back. The reverse, now missing, was described in a contemporary news account as representing ". . . a little fellow carving the name of Henry Clay."

Lent by Mr. and Mrs. Leslie Cowan

10. *John Cummings Edwards* 1804–1888   1844

   Oil on canvas: 35½ x 28½

   Painted in Jefferson City, Missouri; probably in possession of
   subject and inherited by family; Warren V. Patton, Overland,
   Missouri; to present owner, 1958.

REFERENCES: *Jefferson City* (Missouri) *Inquirer*, December 26, 1844, 3–5;
McDermott, pp. 48, 426 (no. 84), ill. Pl. 18.

E.M.B. The contemporary newspaper draws attention to a portrait of
the subject which had been observed in the artist's studio in Jefferson
City at the time, described as being "very perfect indeed." This is in
all probability the portrait referred to by the reporter.

SUBJECT was born in Frankfort, Franklin County, Kentucky, June 24,
1804; died in Stockton, California, October 14, 1888. He graduated
from Black's College in Kentucky, studied law, and was admitted to
the bar in 1825; practiced first in Tennessee and afterward in Missouri,
where he settled. He was Secretary of the State of Missouri from 1830
to 1835 and in 1837; District Judge of Cole County, Missouri, 1832–
1837; member of State House of Representatives, 1836; Judge of State
Supreme Court, 1837–1839. From 1841–1843 he served as a United
States Representative from Missouri; from 1844–1848 as Governor of
Missouri. In 1849 he moved to Stockton, California, where he remained the rest of his life, practicing law, raising cattle, and engaging
in real estate pursuits; was also mayor of Stockton in 1851. (*Biographical
Directory of American Congress, 1774–1961*, House Doc. no. 442, 85th
Congress, 2nd Session, p. 849.)

Lent by the Missouri Historical Society

11. *The Concealed Enemy*   1845

   Oil on canvas: 28½ x 35½

   Submitted by the artist to the American Art-Union, New York, for sale, and purchased at meeting of the institution's committee, December 8, 1845, for $40, described as "Indian Figure-Concealed Enemy"; awarded by the Art-Union at its annual meeting, December 19, 1845, to James A. Hutchison, Pittsburgh, Pennsylvania (no. 95); in later years in the collection of David Ives Bushnell, Jr., Washington, District of Columbia; presented by him to present owner, 1946.

EXHIBITIONS: New York, New York, American Art-Union, 1845 (no. 95); Omaha, Nebraska, Joslyn Art Museum, 1954; St. Louis, Missouri, City Art Museum of St. Louis, 1954 (no. 82); Minneapolis, Minnesota, Walker Art Center, 1955 (no. 82); Kansas City, Missouri, William Rockhill Nelson Gallery of Art, 1961 (no. 5); St. Louis, Missouri, City Art Museum of St. Louis, 1961 (no. 5).

DOCUMENT: Minutes, meeting, committee, American Art-Union, December 8, 1845, coll. New York Historical Society.

REFERENCES: American Art-Union, *Transactions* (1845) (no. 95); Rusk, pp. 33, 120; McDermott, pp. 53, 413 (no. 25), illus. Pl. 20.

Lent by the Peabody Museum of Archaeology and Ethnology, Harvard University

*12. *Cottage Scenery*   1845

Oil on canvas: 25½ x 30. Signed lower left: "G. C. Bingham."

Submitted by the artist to the American Art-Union, New York, for sale; at meeting of committee of the organization, December 8, 1845, a painting entitled "Landscape Cottage," undoubtedly this picture, was purchased for $35; awarded by the Art-Union at its annual meeting, December 19, 1845, to James D. Carhart, Macon, Georgia; in hands of Carhart family until 1960, when it was acquired by Berry-Hill Galleries, New York; purchased by Lawrence A. Fleischman, Detroit, Michigan; then by present owner, 1961.

12. *Cottage Scenery*. 1845

EXHIBITIONS: New York, American Art-Union, 1845 (no. 98); Indianapolis, Indiana, John Herron Art Museum 1961 (no. 4).

DOCUMENT: Minutes, meeting, American Art-Union, December 8, 1845, coll. New York Historical Society.

REFERENCES: American Art-Union, *Transactions* (1845) (no. 98); Rusk, pp. 30, 120; McDermott, pp. 54, 413 (no. 26); E. M. Bloch, "George Caleb Bingham and His Landscape 'Method,' " *Corcoran Bulletin*, XIII (1963), pp. 3–9.

Lent by The Corcoran Gallery of Art, Purchase of Works of Art Fund and Gifts from Charles C. Glover, Jr., The Honorable Orme Wilson, and Mr. and Mrs. Lansdell K. Christie

13. *The Jolly Flatboatmen* (1)   1846

Oil on canvas: 38 x 48½. Signed on boat, lower right: "G. C. Bingham."

Submitted by the artist to the American Art-Union, New York, for sale; recommended for purchase by Union's executive committee, October 9, 1846, for $290, framed, entitled "Dance on the Flat boat"; awarded by the Art-Union at its annual meeting, December 24, 1847, to Benjamin van Schaick, a grocer who resided at 76 Warren St., New York City. According to the present owner's father, Herbert Claiborne Pell (himself a prior owner), the picture is recalled as having been in the family's possession "more than sixty years ago," at that time owned by William Pell, later inherited by his son Clarence Pell, all of New York City (Herbert C. Pell, letter, August 25, 1954, quoted in *Art Quarterly*, XVII [1954], p. 356, n.).

EXHIBITIONS: New York, New York, American Art-Union, 1847 (no. 1); St. Louis, Missouri, City Art Museum of St. Louis, 1954 (no. 150); Minneapolis, Minnesota, Walker Art Center, 1955 (no. 150); Pittsburgh, Pennsylvania, Carnegie Institute, 1957 (no. 23).

DOCUMENT: Minutes, executive committee, American Art-Union, October 9, 1846, coll. New York Historical Society.

REFERENCES: American Art-Union *Transcations* (1847), p. 32 (no. 1); *Literary World*, II (October 23, 1847), 377–378; Rusk, pp. 36, 121; Christ-Janer, p. 35; F. H. Shapley, "Bingham's 'Jolly Flatboatmen'," *Art Quarterly*, XVII (1954), pp. 352–356; McDermott, pp. 56–57, 414 (no. 31), ill. Pl. 22.

Lent by the Honorable Claiborne Pell

Exhibited at Washington only.

*14. *Boatmen on the Missouri*   1846

> Oil on canvas: 25 x 30
>
> Submitted by the artist to the American Art-Union, New York, by May 29, 1846, for sale, and "recommended for purchase"; purchased at meeting of Union's committee of management, July 6, 1846, for $100; at annual meeting of Art-Union, December 18, 1846, awarded to J. R. Macmurdo of New Orleans, Louisiana; by 1905 in collection of John H. Clarke, New Orleans, Louisiana, who, in that year, presented it to Edward Thomas Bergin, Jr., a nephew (d. 1920); inherited by wife (d. 1960); then by grandson, George Bergin, La Jolla, California; sold to Kennedy Galleries, New York, New York, 1966.

EXHIBITION: New York, New York, American Art-Union, 1846 (no. 14)

DOCUMENTS: "Memorandum of pictures to be recommended for purchase," May 29, 1846, American Art-Union, *Letters*, v. 6; minutes, committee of management, American Art-Union, July 6, 1846, coll. New York Historical Society.

REFERENCES: American Art-Union, *Transcactions* (1846), p. 31 (no. 14); Rusk, pp. 37, 121; Christ-Janer, p. 40; McDermott, pp. 54–55, 414 (no. 28); Alfred Frankenstein, "A Lost Masterpiece of American Painting," *San Francisco Chronicle*, June 6, 1966, p. 53.

275–849 O—67——4

14. *Boatman on the Missouri.* 1846.

E.M.B. A copy of this painting, made about 1904, has been for some years in the collection of the Henry Francis du Pont Winterthur Museum, Winterthur, Delaware.

Lent anonymously through the courtesy of the Kennedy Galleries, Inc.

15. *The Wood-Boat*   1850

Oil on canvas: 24¾ x 29⅝

Submitted by the artist to the American Art-Union, New York, for sale, November 19, 1850, for $200, framed, but declined at that time; rejected again at meeting of committee of management, February 20, 1851; purchased at meeting of committee, March 20, 1851, for $125, framed; sold at auction of property of the Art-Union, December 17, 1852, to a Mr. Herrick, for $95; in recent years acquired by John Levy Galleries, New York, from Philip E. Lange, Pittsburgh, Pennsylvania; sold by M. Knoedler and Co., New York, to the present owner, 1951.

EXHIBITIONS: New York, New York, American Art-Union, 1851; San Diego, California, Fine Arts Gallery, 1952; St. Louis, Missouri, City Art Museum of St. Louis, 1954 (no. 158); Minneapolis, Minnesota, Walker Art Center, 1955; Cincinnati, Ohio, Cincinnati Art Museum, 1955 (no. 6); Vancouver, B.C., Canada, Vancouver Art Gallery, 1955; Los Angeles, California, Municipal Art Gallery, 1956; New York, New York, Wildenstein & Co., 1957; New York, New York, American Federation of Arts (Circulating Exhibition), 1958–1959; Kansas City, Missouri, William Rockhill Nelson Gallery of Art, 1961 (no. 10); St. Louis, Missouri, City Art Museum, 1961 (no. 10).

DOCUMENTS: Bingham to American Art-Union, letter, New York, November 19, 1850; Minutes, committee of management, American Art-Union, November 19, 1850, February 20, 1851, March 20, 1851, coll. New York Historical Society.

REFERENCES: American Art-Union *Supplementary Bulletin* series for 1851 (1851) (no. 152); *Catalogue of Pictures and Other Works of Art, the Property of the American Art-Union* (no. 352); Rusk, pp. 51, 122; Christ-Janer, p. 57; *Sunday Post-Dispatch* (St. Louis), July 1, 1951, and July 8, 1951; McDermott, pp. 76–77, 415 (no. 49), ill. Pl. 30.

E.M.B. Contemporary description: "The *'Wood Boat'* is a group such as the traveler daily sees upon the navigable waters of the west. The wood for sale is conveniently placed in a flat boat, while the hardy *choppers* await a purchase in some approaching steamer." [Bingham letter].

Lent by the City Art Museum of St. Louis

Exhibited at Cleveland only.

16. *The Checker Players*   1850

   Oil on canvas: 25 x 30

   Submitted by the artist to the American Art-Union, New York, for sale, January–February 1851, but declined by the committee of management, February 20, 1851; may be identical with picture called "Chess Players" by the reporter who saw it in the artist's studio in Columbia, Missouri, late in October 1851; in possession of N. J. Eaton, St. Louis, Missouri, 1864; in 1952 with The Old Print Shop, New York; sold to present owner, 1952.

EXHIBITIONS: St. Louis, Missouri, Jones's Store, October 1850; St. Louis, Missouri, Fourth Annual Fair of St. Louis Agricultural and Mechanical Association, 1859 (no. 34); St. Louis, Missouri, Mississippi Valley Sanitary Fair, 1864 (no. 192); Cincinnati, Ohio, Cincinnati Art Museum, 1955 (no. 2); Kansas City, Missouri, William Rockhill Nelson Gallery of Art, 1961 (no. 12); City Art Museum of St. Louis, 1961 (no. 12).

DOCUMENTS: Bingham to Rollins, letter, New York, March 30, 1851, coll. State Historical Society of Missouri, Columbia (*M.H.R.*, XXXII

[1937], 21); Minutes, committee of management, American Art-Union, February 20, 1851, coll. New York Historical Society.

REFERENCES: *Missouri Republican* (St. Louis), October 11, 1850; American Art-Union, *Bulletin* (1851), p. 151 (from *Missouri Statesman* [Columbia], October 31, 1851); *Evening Intelligencer* (St. Louis), November 3, 1851; *Inquirer* (Jefferson City), November 15, 1851; Rusk, pp. 54, 122; Christ-Janer, p. 57; E. P. Richardson, " 'The Checker Players' by George Caleb Bingham," *Art Quarterly*, XV (1952), pp. 252–256; McDermott, pp. 78–79, 416 (no. 52), ill. Pl. 29.

E.M.B. The painting was entitled "Game of Draughts" when it was on exhibition in St. Louis in 1859 and 1864.

Lent by The Detroit Institute of Arts

Gift of Dexter M. Ferry, Jr.

17. *Mississippi Boatman*   1850

    Oil on canvas: 24 x 17½. Signed and dated, lower left: "G. C. Bingham/1850"

    Submitted to the Philadelphia Art-Union and exhibited there, in accordance with the plan of that organization, listed for sale at $60; subsequent history unknown until its discovery and acquisition by present owner, circa 1964.

EXHIBITION: Philadelphia, Pennsylvania, Philadelphia Art-Union, 1851 (no. 51).

DOCUMENT: Bingham to Rollins, letter, New York, March 30, 1851, coll. State Historical Society of Missouri, Columbia (*M.H.R.*, XXXII [1937], 21).

REFERENCES: Philadelphia Art-Union, *Reporter*, I (January 1851), no. 51; Philadelphia Art-Union, *Catalogue of Prizes to be Distributed on December 31, 1852;* McDermott, p. 416 (no. 58).

E.M.B. Contemporary description: "An old man smoking his morning pipe, at the Riverside." [*Reporter*, January 1851.]

Lent by John Wilmerding

18. *Shooting for the Beef* 1850

    Oil on canvas: 33½ x 49¼. Signed and dated, lower left: "G. C. Bingham/1850."

    Completed by June, 1850, when a daguerreotype was made of it by W. Benson (Private coll.). Probably painted at St. Louis, Missouri, reportedly commissioned by George W. Austen, treasurer of the American Art-Union, New York, but actually submitted by the artist to the institution itself, February 1, 1851, for sale at $350, unframed, and purchased for that amount after March 20, 1851; sold at auction of the property of the Art-Union, December 16, 1852, to Isaac Townsend for $190; in January 1935, with C. W. Lyon, Inc., New York; later in the collection of Stephen C. Clark, New York; passed to collection of Francis P. Garvan and was part of his estate on loan at Yale University, New Haven, Connecticut; afterward with C. W. Lyon, Inc ; sold to present owner by the Macbeth Gallery, New York, 1940.

EXHIBITIONS: St. Louis, Missouri, Jone's Store, October, 1850; New York, New York, American Art-Union, by December, 1851 (no. 173); New York, New York, Museum of Modern Art, 1935 (no. 7); Hartford, Connecticut, Wadsworth Atheneum, 1935 (no. 7); New York, New York, Whitney Museum of American Art, 1935 (no. 7); San Francisco, California, M. H. de Young Memorial Museum, 1935 (sec. 1, no. 66); New York, New York, Metropolitan Museum of Art, 1939 (no. 135); Boston, Massachusetts, Museum of Fine Arts, 1944 (no. 14); Milwaukee, Wisconsin, Milwaukee Art Institute, 1947 (no. 11); Kansas City, Missouri, William Rockhill Nelson Gallery of Art, 1950; New York, New York, National Academy of

Design, 1951 (no. 7); St. Louis, Missouri, City Art Museum of St. Louis, 1954 (no. 157); Minneapolis, Minnesota, Walker Art Center, 1955 (no. 157).

DOCUMENTS: American Art-Union, Register of Works of Art, February 1, 1851; Minutes, meeting, American Art-Union, March 20, 1851, coll. New York Historical Society.

REFERENCES: *Missouri Republican* (St. Louis), June 4, Oct. 11, 1850; American Art-Union, *Bulletin* (July, 1850), pp. 64–65; ibid. (December, 1850), p. 157; ibid. (December 1851); *Catalogue of Pictures and Other Works of Art, the Property of the American Art-Union* (no. 221); Rusk, pp. 49–50, 122; Christ-Janer, pp. 54–55, ill. Pl. VI, no. 2; McDermott, pp. 74–75, 415 (no. 47), ill. Pl. 28.

Lent by The Brooklyn Museum

Exhibited at Washington and Cleveland only.

19. *The Storm*   circa 1850

Oil on canvas: 25⅛ x 30¹⁄₁₆

Discovered in an antique shop in St. Louis, Missouri, by Oscar Thalinger, 1934; sold by him to Meyric R. Rogers, St. Louis, Missouri (later of Chicago, Illinois); with M. Knoedler & Co., New York, 1944; purchased by Henry E. Schnakenberg, New York (later of Newtown, Connecticut), December 1944; presented by him to current owner, 1952.

EXHIBITIONS: St. Louis, Missouri, City Art Museum of St. Louis, 1934; Kansas City, Missouri, William Rockhill Nelson Gallery of Art, 1934; New York, New York, Museum of Modern Art, 1935 (no. 16); Hartford, Connecticut, Wadsworth Atheneum, 1935 (no. 16); Springfield, Massachusetts, Springfield Museum of Art, 1938; New York, New York, M. Knoedler & Co., 1944 (no. 3); New York, New York, Brooklyn Museum, 1945; Hagerstown, Maryland, Washington County Museum of Fine Arts, 1947 (no. 3); St. Louis, Missouri, City Art Museum of St. Louis, 1954 (no. 18); Minneapolis, Minnesota, Walker Art Center, 1955 (no. 18); Kansas City, Missouri, William Rockhill Nelson Gallery of Art, 1961 (no. 19); St. Louis, Missouri, City Art Museum of St. Louis, 1961 (no. 19).

REFERENCES: Wadsworth Atheneum, *Bulletin*, series 2, no. 33 (May, 1952); McDermott, pp. 117, 418 (no. 75), ill. Pl. 50.

Lent by the Wadsworth Atheneum

Gift of Henry Schnakenberg

20. *Mississippi Fisherman*   circa 1850

    Oil on canvas: 29½ x 24½

In possession of family of artist's second wife, Mrs. William P. Thomas; inherited by Mrs. Andrew T. Caldwell, Lake Charles, Louisiana; with James Graham & Sons, New York, 1961; acquired by present owner, 1963.

Lent by Mr. and Mrs. Marshall Field

21. *Landscape With Deer*   circa 1850

    Oil on canvas: 24¾ x 30

Said to have been purchased from the artist by Charles W. Peck and inherited by daughter, Mrs. J. Warren Dusenbery (Rebecca Peck), St. Louis, Missouri (letter, C. van Ravenswaay to E. Maurice Bloch, March 7, 1956); bequest to present owner, 1947.

REFERENCE: McDermott, pp. 118, 418 (no. 79), ill. Pl. 54.

E.M.B. One of a pair of landscapes by the artist in the same collection, from the same source.

Lent by the Missouri Historical Society

22. *Thomas Hart Benton 1782–1858*   After 1850

Oil on canvas: 30 x 25

In possession of Mrs. B. B. Graham and given by her to present owner in 1905.

REFERENCES: Missouri Historical Society, *Bulletin*, V (1949), p. 229; ibid., XIII (1957), p. 339; McDermott, p. 427 (no. 105).

E.M.B. Another (?) portrait of the subject was reportedly destroyed in the fire in the Capitol, Jefferson City, Missouri, February 5, 1911 (C. B. Rollins, *Missouri Historical Review*, XXXIII [1939], pp. 325–326).

SUBJECT was the American statesman, born in Orange County, North Carolina, March 14, 1782; died April 10, 1858. Lived in Tennessee with his family as a youth, later entered the study of law and was admitted to the bar in 1811. Elected to the Tennessee State Legislature. During War of 1812 served as aide-de-camp to Andrew Jackson; appointed a lieutenant colonel in regular army. Moved to St. Louis in 1815, practiced law and established a newspaper there. Upon the admission of Missouri to Union in 1820, he was elected a senator; afterward reelected every term for thirty years. (*Encyclopedia Americana*, III, pp. 520–524.)

Lent by the Missouri Historical Society

23. *The Emigration of Daniel Boone* or *Daniel Boone Escorting a Band of Pioneers Into the Western Country*   1851

Oil on canvas: 36½ x 50

Painted in New York City; begun by March 1851. Submitted to American Art-Union, New York for purchase, received April 14, 1851, declined. "In charge of Mr. Philips, the Piano forte merchant" (Nathaniel Phillips), in St. Louis, March 1853. The artist proposed to dispose of the picture by raffle (*Missouri Statesman*

[Columbia], October 29, 1852). "The painting was sold to a man in Boston by the Federals during the [Civil] War after its confiscation at an auction house on Fourth Street, in St. Louis" (Bryan Obear to Jesse P. Crump, letter, St. Louis, October 23, 1918). The present owner's records state that the picture was presented to the university in 1890 by Nathaniel Phillips of Boston, Massachusetts.

EXHIBITIONS: Exhibited by the artist in St. Louis, June, 1853; Columbia Missouri, University of Missouri, 1910 (no. 16); St. Louis, Missouri, City Art Museum of St. Louis, 1934 (no. 8); New York, New York, Museum of Modern Art, 1935 (no. 9); Hartford, Connecticut, Wadsworth Atheneum (no. 9); New York, New York, Metropolitan Museum of Art, 1939 (no. 79); New York, New York, Museum of Modern Art, 1943 (no. 27); Philadelphia, Pennsylvania, Pennsylvania Academy of the Fine Arts, 1955 (no. 49); Kansas City, Missouri, William Rockhill Nelson Gallery of Art, 1961 (no. 14); St. Louis, Missouri, City Art Museum of St Louis, 1961 (no. 14).

DOCUMENTS: Bingham to Rollins, letters, coll. State Historical Society of Missouri, Columbia; New York, March 30, 1851; St. Louis, March 9, 1853; Philadelphia, October 3, 1853, February 1, 1854, May 29, 1854 (*Missouri Historical Review* XXXII [1937–38], pp. 21, 29, 165, 178, 185); Obear to Crump, letter, Kansas City Public Library, Kansas City, Missouri; Register of Pictures, American Art-Union, coll. New York Historical Society.

REFERENCES: *Missouri Statesman* (Columbia), May 23, 1851, 3–1 (from *St. Louis Republican*, May 13); October 29, 1852, 2–5; June 17, 1853; *Weekly Missouri Sentinel* (Columbia), October 28, 1852; *Weekly Tribune* (Glasgow), November 11, 1852 (reprinted in *Glasgow Missourian*, September 10, 1936); Rust, pp. 51–53, 122, ill. Pl. XXV; Christ-Janer, pp. 58–59, ill. Pl. VI, no. 1; McDermott, pp. 84–86, 416 (no. 61), ill. Pl. 36.

E.M.B. A copy of the painting, by W. F. Hardy (dates unknown) of St. Louis, is owned by the Daniel Boone Hotel, Columbia, Missouri.

Lent by Washington University

24. *In a Quandary* or *Mississippi Raftmen at Cards*   1851

Oil on canvas: 17¼ x 21. Signed and dated, lower left: "G. C. Bingham/1851."

Probably painted in New York, commissioned by Goupil & Co.; in recent times in the Francis P. Garvan collection, Yale University, New Haven, Connecticut; on market, New York; sold to Mrs. Paul Moore, Convent, New Jersey; given to her son, the present owner.

EXHIBITIONS: New York, New York, Metropolitan Museum of Art, 1939 (no. 133); Washington, District of Columbia, Corcoran Gallery of Art, 1960 (no. 116).

DOCUMENT: Bingham to Rollins, letter, New York, March 30, 1851, coll. State Historical Society of Missouri, Columbia (*Missouri Historical Review*, XXXII [1937], p. 21).

REFERENCES: Rusk, pp. 42, 121; Christ-Janer, pp. 41–42; J. F. McDermott, "The Quandary about Bingham's 'In a Quandary' and 'Raftsmen Playing Cards,'" *Bulletin City Art Museum of St. Louis*, XLII (1957), pp. 6–9; McDermott, pp. 52, 80–81, 189, 416 (no. 59), illus. Pl. 32.

E.M.B. The smaller version of the subject, probably painted specifically in connection with the lithograph published by Goupil & Co. Rusk dates the picture "1847 (by)" and confuses it with the larger picture awarded by the American Art-Union to E. Croswell of Albany, New York, which was actually the version now owned by the City Art Museum of St. Louis, and at the time of her writing in the collection of the "Atheneum Museum," Pittsfield, Massachusetts. Both Rusk and Christ-Janer seek to identify the smaller version with the picture described in an 1847 newspaper.

Lent by Paul Moore, Jr.

Exhibited at Washington and Cleveland only.

*25. *Landscape: Mountain View*   After 1851

Oil on canvas: 21 x 30. Signed lower left: "G.C. Bingham."

In recent years acquired by William D. Sage, East Lansing, Michigan; with Harry Shaw Newman Gallery (The Old Print Shop), New York, 1946–1947; sold to present owner by Victor D. Spark, New York, 1965.

REFERENCES: *Panorma*, II (1947), p. 60, illus. cover, entitled "Landscape on the Upper Mississippi"; McDermott, pp. 117, 418 (no. 76), ill. Pl. 51.

Lent by the Los Angeles County Museum of Art

*26. *Canvassing for a Vote* or *Candidate Electioneering*   1851/1852

Oil on canvas: 25⅛ x 30³⁄₁₆. Signed and dated, lower left: "G.C. Bingham/1852."

Probably painted at Columbia and St. Louis, Missouri, commissioned by Goupil & Co. (M. Knoedler), New York, by March 1851; in later years owned by the McIntyre family; Dr. Elwyn Evans, Orlando Beach, Florida; sold to present owner, 1954.

EXHIBITIONS: Cincinnati, Ohio, Cincinnati Art Museum, 1955 (no. 1); Kansas City, Missouri, William Rockhill Nelson Gallery of Art, 1961 (no. 16); St. Louis, Missouri, City Art Museum of St. Louis, 1961 (no. 16).

DOCUMENTS: Bingham to Rollins, letter, New York, March 30, 1851, coll. State Historical Society of Missouri, Columiba (*Missouri Historical*

25. *Landscape: Mountain View.* After 1851.

26. *Canvassing for a Vote* or *Candidate Electioneering.* 1851/1852.

Review, XXXII [1937], p. 21); Bingham to Goupil & Co., letter, St. Louis, Missouri, January 31, 1852, coll. M. Knoedler & Co., New York.

REFERENCES: *Missouri Statesman* (Columbia), October 31, 1851, 2-1 (copied in American Art Union, *Bulletin* [December 1851], p. 151); *New-York Mirror*, September, 1852 (copied in *Missouri Statesman*, September 10, 1852, pp. 1-7); Rusk, pp. 53-54, 122; Christ-Janer, p. 70; *Kansas City Star*, October 31, 1954; *Missouri Historical Review*, XLIX (1955), p. 189; R.E. Taggart, " 'Canvassing for a Vote' and Some Unpublished Portraits by Bingham" *Art Quarterly*, XVIII (1955), pp. 229-240, illus., Fig. 1; McDermott, pp. 87-88, 417 (no. 65), illus. Pl. 38.

E.M.B. The painting may have been executed specifically in connection with the lithograph published afterward by Goupil & Co. There is also a copy of this subject, at one time attributed to Bingham, but undoubtedly made after the lithograph by another hand.

Lent by the Nelson Gallery-Atkins Museum, Nelson Fund

27. *Woodboatmen On a River*   1854

Oil on canvas: 29 x 36. Signed and dated, lower left: "G. C. Bingham/1854."

Possibly painted in Philadelphia, Pennsylvania; afterward in possession of Col. J. L. D. Morrison, St. Louis, Missouri; purchased by Charles Holmes, circa 1865; sold to Alfred Clifford, circa 1885; inherited by Oliver M. Clifford in 1927; with Max Safron, New York, 1944; sold to Maxim Karolik, Newport, Rhode Island, 1945; included in gift of M. and M. Karolik Collection to present owner, 1949. (Early provenance, letters, O. M. Clifford to E. Maurice Bloch, July 5, 1944, and April 14, 1945.)

REFERENCES: *M. and M. Karolik Collection of American Paintings, 1815 to 1865* (Published for the Museum of Fine Arts, Boston, Massachusetts;

Harvard University Press, 1949), pp. 108–110 (no. 55), illus. opp. p. 109; McDermott, pp. 114, 418 (no. 82), illus. Pl. 48.

Lent by the Museum of Fine Arts, Boston, M. and M. Karolik Collection

*28. *The Verdict of the People* (*2*)   After 1855

     Oil on canvas: 22⅞ x 30⅜ (after transference, 1944). Originally painted on academy board: 24; x 29¾.

     Collection of the artist; included in the artist's estate, September 1879 (no. 3), appraised at $500, purchased at administrator's sale of the Bingham estate, held at Findlay's Art Store, Kansas City, Missouri, March 25, 1893, by James W. S. Peters of Kansas City, for $200; still in collection in 1940; later with Findlay Art Galleries (Walstein C. Findlay), Kansas City, Missouri; to Mc-Caughen & Burr (C. Burr McCaughen), St. Louis, Missouri, 1944; to John Levy Gallery, New York, 1944; purchased by Joseph Katz, Baltimore, Maryland, 1944; with M. Knoedler & Co., New York; sold to present owner.

Exhibitions:Kansas City, Missouri, Kansas City Art Institute, 1909; Columbia, Missouri, University of Missouri, 1910 (no. 10); Kansas City, Missouri, Kansas City Museum, 1914 (no. 4); Memphis, Tennessee, Brooks Memorial Art Gallery, 1945 (no. 15).

References: *Kansas City Star*, March 18, 1893, 5–1; March 25, 1893, 1–6; *Kansas City Journal*, March 25, 1893, 3–1; March 26, 1893, 2–4; Rusk, pp. 62–63, 122, illus. Pl. XXXII; Christ-Janer, p. 86; McDermott, pp. 162–163, 420 (no. 107), illus. Pl. 78.

E.M.B. Dated 1878 by McDermott (pp. 162–163), chiefly on the basis of a contemporary newspaper account in which this painting was included among others said to be "just finished" and on view in the artist's Columbia studio early in 1879 (St. Louis *Republican*, February 9, 1879 and Columbia *Missouri Statesman*, March 7, 1879, from Colum-

28. *The Verdict of the People* (2). After 1855.

bia *Herald*). Since the article reveals several errors in reporting known facts about several of the paintings mentioned, such documentation must obviously be regarded as totally unreliable. The other basis for the dating put forward by McDermott is no longer supportable. Stylistic evidence seems to point much more convincingly to the period in which the first version of the subject was produced, an evaluation first made by Rusk, who dated the painting "after 1854." A smaller and altered version of the subject painted 1854–1855 and now in the collection of the Boatmen's National Bank of St. Louis. Damages upper right and foreground, restored 1944.

Lent by The R. W. Norton Art Gallery

*29. *Jolly Flatboatmen in Port*   1857

    Oil on canvas: 47½ x 69½

    Painted in Düsseldorf, Germany; begun before June, completed by late October 1857; still in the hands of the artist in 1860 and placed by him on indefinite loan to The St. Louis Mercantile Library Association in 1862; purchased 1865 by John How, probably intended for the O'Fallon Polytechnic Institute of St. Louis, of which he was president; removed from the library by How in 1867; in all probability returned to the library between 1868 and 1879; presented to the institution by John H. Beach in 1879; on loan to the City Art Museum of St. Louis, 1934–1944; sold to the present owner, 1944.

EXHIBITIONS: Washington, District of Columbia, Washington Art Association, 1860 (no. 9); St. Louis, Missouri, Western Academy of Art, 1860 (no. 12); Philadelphia, Pennsylvania, Pennsylvania Academy of the Fine Arts, 1860 (no. 141); St. Louis, Missouri, St. Louis Fair and Exposition, 1879 (no. 329); Chicago, Illinois, World's Columbian Exposition, 1893 (Gr. 146, no. 2804c); St. Louis, Missouri, City Art Museum of St. Louis, 1934 (no. 12); Kansas City, Missouri, William

29. *Jolly Flatboatmen in Port.* 1857.

Rockhill Nelson Gallery of Art, 1934; New York, New York, Museum of Modern Art, 1935 (no. 13); Hartford, Connecticut, Wadsworth Atheneum, 1935; Davenport, Iowa, Davenport Art Museum, 1941; Dallas, Texas, Dallas Museum of Fine Arts, 1946 (no. 8); Denver, Colorado, Denver Art Museum, 1948; Columbus, Ohio, Columbus Museum of Art, 1948; St. Louis, Missouri, City Art Museum of St. Louis, 1949 (no. 18); Denver, Colorado, Denver Art Museum, 1951; New York, New York, American Academy of Arts and Letters, 1954 (no. 157); Philadelphia, Pennsylvania, Pennsylvania Academy of the Fine Arts, 1955 (no. 50); Kansas City, Missouri, William Rockhill Nelson Gallery of Art, 1961 (no. 25); St. Louis, Missouri, City Art Museum of St. Louis, 1961 (no. 25).

DOCUMENTS: Bingham to Rollins, letters, Düsseldorf, June 3 and October 12, 1857, coll. State Historical Society of Missouri, Columbia (*M.H.R.*, XXXII [1938], p. 357).

REFERENCES: *Weekly Missouri Statesman* (Columbia), December 18, 1857, 3–3; *Liberty* (Missouri) *Weekly Tribune*, December 18, 1857, 2–1; Board of Directors, Mercantile Library Association of St. Louis, *Seventeenth Annual Report* (January 13, 1863), p. 18; *Twentieth Annual Report* (1865), p. 22; *Twenty-second Annual Report* (1867), p. 14; *Thirty-fourth Annual Report* (1879), pp. 18–19; City Art Museum (St. Louis), *Bulletin*, IX (1924), p. 60 (Mary Powell); ibid., XIX (1934), p. 20 (Meyric R. Rogers); Christ-Janer, pp. 91–95, illus. Pl. XI, no. 1; McDermott, pp. 124–125, 419 (no. 86), illus. Pl. 35; Rusk, pp. 68–69, 123. Lent by the City Art Museum of St. Louis.

*30. *Dr. Benoist Troost* 1786–1859   1859
    Oil on canvas: 40½ x 29⅝

    Probably painted in Kansas City, Missouri; owned by subject and his wife; later in the possession of Dr. David Rittenhouse Porter (1838–1916), who "attended Mrs. Troost in her last illness";

30. *Dr. Benoist Troost.* 1859.

given by him to the Board of Education, Kansas City, Missouri, in 1905; presented by the Board to the current owner, 1935. (Pierre R. Porter to E. Maurice Bloch, letter, Kansas City, January 2, 1945.)

EXHIBITIONS: Kansas City, Missouri, Missouri Valley Historical Society, 1914 (no. 2); St. Louis, Missouri, City Art Museum of St. Louis, 1934 (no. 13); New York, New York, Museum of Modern Art, 1935 (no. 14); Hartford, Connecticut, Wadsworth Atheneum, 1935 (no. 14); Kansas City, Missouri, William Rockhill Nelson Gallery of Art, 1953; Pittsburgh, Pennsylvania, Carnegie Institute, 1957 (no. 22); Kansas City, Missouri, William Rockhill Nelson Gallery of Art, 1961 (no. 26); St. Louis, Missouri, City Art Museum of St. Louis, 1961 (no. 26).

REFERENCES: Rusk, pp. 70–71, 123; *Kansas City Star*, May 6, 1935; Christ-Janer, pp. 96–97, illus. Pl. XII, no. 1; McDermott, pp. 128, 428 (no. 133), illus. Pl. 57.

E.M.B. A companion portrait of Mrs. Benoist Troost (Mary Gillis) is in the same collection.

SUBJECT was born in Bois LeDuc, Holland, November 17, 1786; died Kansas City, Missouri, February 8, 1859. He is said to have arrived in America before 1845, settling first in Pittsburg, Pennsylvania, and St. Louis, Missouri, before coming to Kansas City. He was the first physician to locate on the present site of that city. (C. W. Whitney, *Kansas City, Missouri: Its History and Its People*, I, pp. 472–473.)

Lent by the Nelson Gallery—Atkins Museum
Gift of the Board of Education of Kansas City, Missouri

*31. *Martial Law* or *Order No. 11* (1)   1865–1869

    Oil on canvas: 55½ x 78½

    Painted at Independence, Missouri; begun by November 1865, completed probably January 1869; collection of the artist; in-

31. *Martial Law* or *Order No. 11* (*1*). 1865–1869.

cluded in inventory of his estate, September 1879 (no. 1), appraised at $250; in administrator's sale of the Bingham estate, Findlay's Art Store, Kansas City, Missouri, March 25, 1893, reportedly purchased by J.W.S. Peters, for $675, who was probably acting for Col. Joseph Wayne Mercer, Independence, Missouri; inherited by his wife, Laura Greene Mercer; then by Mrs. Walter Brown, Kansas City, Missouri; on deposit with William Rockhill Nelson Gallery of Art, Kansas City; purchased by David B. Findlay (Findlay Art Gallery), New York, 1947; acquired by present owner, 1958.

EXHIBITIONS: St. Louis, Missouri, Pettes and Leathe's Gallery, 1869; New York, New York, Knoedler Galleries, 1952; Cincinnati, Ohio, Cincinnati Art Museum, 1958 (no. 21).

DOCUMENT: Copyright for the painting, registered in the Western District of Missouri (no. 52), December 22, 1868, coll. Kansas City (Missouri) Musuem.

REFERENCES: *Missouri Statesman* (Columbia), November 24, 1865 (from *Kansas City Journal*); *Jefferson City* (Missouri) *People's Tribune*, December 23, 1868, 1–4 (from *Independence Sentinel*); *Missouri Statesman* (Columbia), January 1, 1869, 3–2; *Saline County Progress*, March 19, 1869, 1–4; *Jefferson City* (Missouri) *People's Tribune*, March 24, 1869, 1–4; *Daily Missouri Democrat* (St. Louis), June 6, 1869, 1; *Kansas City Star*, March 18, 1893, 5–1; March 25, 1893, 1–6; *Kansas City Journal*, March 25, 1893, 3–1; March 26, 1893, 2–4; Rusk, pp. 82–84, 107, 124; Christ-Janer, pp. 102–104; McDermott, pp. 139–140, 419 (no. 994).

E.M.B. This is the earlier of the two versions of the subject painted by the artist; the second version (circa 1869–1870) is in the collection of the State Historical Society of Missouri, Columbia. The two versions differ only in minor details, and only slightly in size. The engraving by John Sartain, produced in 1872, is after the second version.

Lent by the Cincinnati Art Museum

66

*32. *General Francis Preston Blair, Jr.* 1821–1875   1871

    Oil on canvas: 34 x 29. Signed, lower left: "G.C. Bingham."

    Painted in Kansas City, Missouri; said to have been in the posses-
sion of Mrs. James M. Piper of Kansas City, in 1902 (Rollins
Bingham to Miss May Simonds, letter, June 18, 1902; Rusk, p. 91);
Mrs. Frank P. Blair III, Chicago, Illinois, by 1917; Mrs. Edward
Henrotin (Emily Blair), Cherry Plain, New York; sold to present
owner.

DOCUMENT: Bingham to Rollins, letter, Kansas City, March 6, 1871
(*M.H.R.*, XXXIII [1938], p. 67).

REFERENCES: Rusk, pp. 90–91, 125; McDermott, pp. 152, 431 (no. 179).

E.M.B. A study for the full-length portrait that was at one time in the
collection of The St. Louis Mercantile Library Association, and now,
in a reduced state, in the Missouri Historical Society, St. Louis.
Dated circa 1869 by Rusk, but documentation definitely places the
portrait in the later period.

Lent by Hirschl & Adler Galleries, Inc.

33. *Major James Sidney Rollins* 1812–1888   1871

    Oil on canvas: 30 x 25

    Painted at Columbia, Missouri; in possession of subject and his
wife; inherited by their son, George Bingham Rollins; given to
present owner in 1961 by his heirs; James S. Rollins II and James S.
Rollins III; all of Columbia, Missouri.

EXHIBITIONS: Columbia, Missouri, University of Missouri, 1910 (no.
34); St. Louis, Missouri, City Art Museum of St. Louis, 1934 (no.
17); New York, New York, Museum of Modern Art, 1935 (no. 17);
Hartford, Connecticut, Wadsworth Atheneum, 1935 (no. 17).

REFERENCES: *Missouri Statesman* (Columbia), October 13, 1871, 3–3;

32. *General Francis Preston Blair, Jr.* 1871.

Rusk, pp. 94, 125, illus. Pl. XLVII; Christ-Janer, p. 111, ill. Pl. XIV, no. 1; McDermott, pp. 154, 431 (no. 187); *M.H.R.*, LVI (1962), pp. 115–116.

E.M.B. A portrait from life, undoubtedly intended as a model for the head of a life-size, full-length portrait that was commissioned by the subject's friends for presentation to the University of Missouri. The full-length portrait was destroyed during the fire at the University in 1892, but a preparatory study (33 x 30) for the design is now in the collection of Mr. David Westfall, Columbia, Missouri. Another portrait, from 1834, is held in the estate of Curtis Burnam Rollins, Columbia, Missouri.

SUBJECT was born in Richmond, Madison County, Kentucky, April 19, 1812, son of Dr. Anthony Wayne and Sarah (Sallie) Harris (Rodes) Rollins; died Columbia, Missouri, January 9, 1888. He married Mary Elizabeth Hickman at Columbia, June 6, 1837. His was an active life in state and national politics; a candidate of the Whig Party for the governorship of his state, 1848; candidate of the Free Party for governor, 1857; served in State Senate, 1846; U.S. Senator from Missouri, 1860. He was the artist's best friend, patron, and benefactor.

Lent by the State Historical Society of Missouri

34. *Miss Vinnie Ream* 1847–1914   1876
Oil on canvas: 40 x 30. Signed, lower center: "G. C. Bingham."

Painted in Washington, District of Columbia, probably March-April 1876; in possession of subject and inherited by her husband, General Richard Leveridge Hoxie; presented to current owner by the second Mrs. Hoxie, 1929.

EXHIBITIONS: St. Louis, Missouri, City Art Museum of St. Louis, 1934 (no. 18); New York, New York, Museum of Modern Art, 1935 (no. 18); Hartford, Connecticut, Wadsworth Atheneum, 1935 (no. 18);

Kansas City, Missouri, William Rockhill Nelson Gallery of Art, 1961 (no. 38); St. Louis, Missouri, City Art Museum of St. Louis, 1961 (no. 38).

Document: Bingham to Rollins, letter, Washington, District of Columbia, April 13, 1876, coll. State Historical Society of Missouri, Columbia (*M.H.R.*, XXXIII [1938], pp. 363–364).

References: *Kansas City* (Missouri) *Times*, April 29, 1876; *The Daily Tribune* (Jefferson City, Missouri), April 30, 1876, 2–1; May 10, 1876, 1–4; Rusk, pp. 100, 125; *Missouri Magazine*, October 26, 1929; *M.H.R.*, XXIV (1930), pp. 288–289; XXXIII (1938), p. 364, n. 15; Christ-Janer, pp. 117–118, illus. Pl. XII, no. 2; McDermott, pp. 155, 431 (no. 191).

Subject was born Madison, Wisconsin, Sept. 25, 1847, the daughter of Robert Lee and Lavinia (McDonald) Ream; died Nov. 20, 1914. She came to Washington, D.C. with her family when a child. The family later moved west and she was educated at Christian College in Columbia, Missouri. After working for a time as a clerk in the Post Office Department, she gave up her position to study art, devoting her attention to sculpture, studying under Bonnat at Paris and Majoli in Rome. She was the first woman to receive a commission from Congress under which she executed the statue of Abraham Lincoln, now in the rotunda of the Capitol; later Congress commissioned the statue of Admiral Farragut, now standing in Farragut Square in Washington. She also modeled portrait busts and medallions of Lincoln, Thaddeus Stevens, John Sherman, Ezra Cornell, Horace Greeley, Peter Cooper, General U. S. Grant, General George B. McClellan, and others. She married, May 28, 1878, Richard Leveridge Hoxie (later a brigadier general). (R. L. Hoxie, comp., *Vinnie Ream*.)

Lent by the State Historical Society of Missouri

*35. *Self-Portrait of the Artist* 1811–1879   circa 1877

Oil on canvas: 26½ x 21½

In all probability the painting included in the administrator's sale of the Bingham estate held at Findlay's Store, Kansas City, Missouri, March 25, 1893, purchased by Thomas H. Mastin for $45.

EXHIBITIONS: Kansas City, Missouri, Missouri Valley Historical Society, 1914 (no. 1); St Louis, Missouri, City Art Museum of St. Louis, 1934 (no. 20); Kansas City, Missouri, William Rockhill Nelson Gallery of Art, 1953 (no. 140); Kansas City, Missouri, William Rockhill Nelson Gallery of Art, 1961 (no. 39); St. Louis, Missouri, City Art Museum of St. Louis, 1961 (no. 39).

REFERENCES: *Kansas City Star*, March 18, 1893, 5–1; March 25, 1893, 1–6; *Kansas City Journal*, March 25, 1893, 3–1; March 26, 1893, 2–4; Rusk, pp. 106, 126, illus. frontis.; Christ-Janer, p. 129, illus. Pl.-XIV, no. 2; McDermott, pp. 154, 432 (no. 199), illus. Pl. 67.

Lent by the Kansas City Public Library, Kansas City, Missouri

DRAWINGS

All but one of the drawings included in this exhibition are lent from the collection of The St. Louis Mercantile Library Association. The complete collection, numbering 112 drawings, was given to the Library in 1868 by John How, then president of the O'Fallon Polytechnic Institute of St. Louis. Apparently, Mr. How got them from the artist at the same time he acquired the three paintings comprising the Election Series, and the *Jolly Flatboatmen in Port*.

Until recently the drawings were mounted and bound in album form. In the listing below, the initials ML, followed by a number, indicate the order in which the drawings originally appeared in the album. That order was obviously not based on a system related to finished compositions. This fact suggests that the album served the artist as a model-book, to be drawn upon as new compositions were begun. For the purposes of this catalog, however, the drawings are grouped together in relationship to the paintings in which they first appeared.

The majority of the drawings can be associated with known paintings executed by Bingham between 1845 and 1857, a period which also marks his major efforts in the field of narrative painting.

All the drawings are executed in pencil, brush and ink, gray wash, heightened with white.

E.M.B.

36. Fur-trader's Son: for *Fur Traders Descending the Missouri*, 1845

Album no. ML26. 6⅞ x 10

Boy, reclining, turned toward right, looking out to observer, left hand held against side of head; rifle-beneath him. Figure also used in second version of subject, *Trappers' Return*, 1851. Also adapted, with alterations, for *Jolly Flatboatmen in Port*, 1857.

ILLUSTRATIONS: Christ-Janer, Figure 6; McDermott, p. 280 (no. 2)

REFERENCES: Christ-Janer, p. 37; McDermott, p. 53.

37. Fur Trader: for *Fur Traders Descending the Missouri*, 1845

Album no. ML35. 11⅞ x 9½.

Man seated in dugout, turned toward left, looking out to observer; holds paddle. The same figure used by the artist in his second version of the subject, *Trappers' Return*, 1851.

ILLUSTRATIONS: Rusk, Pl. XV, l.r.; Metropolitan Museum of Art, *Bulletin*, vol. XXVIII (1933), p. 122; Christ-Janer, Figure 5; McDermott, p. 279 (no. 1).

REFERENCES: Christ-Janer, p. 37; McDermott, p. 53.

38. Skillet-beater: for *The Jolly Flatboatmen* (1), 1846

Album no. ML10.   10¼ x 9⅜

Young man seated, facing observer, turned slightly to right, beating time on skillet; *verso:* sketch of head.

ILLUSTRATIONS: Christ-Janer, Figure 2; McDermott, p. 282 (no. 4).

REFERENCES: Christ-Janer, pp. 35–36; McDermott, pp. 57, 124.

39. Fiddler: for *The Jolly Flatboatmen* (1), 1846

Album no. ML11.   10⅛ x 8⅛

Man seated on barrel, turned toward left, playing fiddle. Similar, with slight variations, to ML2; *verso:* sketches of two landscapes.

ILLUSTRATIONS: Christ-Janer, Figure 1 (*recto*); McDermott, p. 283 (no. 5) (*recto*); *George Caleb Bingham, Sesquicentennial Exhibition* . . . (The Nelson Gallery and Atkins Museum, *Bulletin*, vol. III), p. [26] (*verso*).

REFERENCES: Christ-Janer, p. 35; McDermott, pp. 57, 124.

40. Flatboatman: for *The Jolly Flatboatmen* (1), 1846

Album no. ML14.   10 x 8¼

Man reclining, back to observer, hands clasped behind head. The same figure used by artist in later version of subject, *The Jolly Flatboatmen* (2), *circa* 1848.

ILLUSTRATION: McDermott, p. 285 (no. 7).

REFERENCE: McDermott, p. 57.

41. Flatboatman: for *The Jolly Flatboatmen* (1), 1846

Album no. ML23.   9¾ x 7¾

Man seated on raft pole, turned toward left, looking out to observer; *verso:* light sketch of figure.

ILLUSTRATIONS: Rusk, Pl. XX, top; Christ-Janer, Figure 3; McDermott, p. 286 (no. 8).

REFERENCES: Rusk, p. 36; Christ-Janer, p. 36; McDermott, p. 57.

42. Flatboatman: for *The Jolly Flatboatmen* (1), 1846

Album no. ML55. 10 x 8

Man seated, turned toward right, seen partly from back; looks back over right shoulder to observer.

ILLUSTRATIONS: Christ-Janer, Figure 4; McDermott, p. 287 (no.9).

REFERENCES: Christ-Janer, p. 36; McDermott, p. 67.

43. Boatman: for *The Jolly Flatboatmen* (1), 1846

Album no. ML47. 9 x 9⅞

Man seated on setting pole, back turned to observer; right arm rests on raised right leg, hand raised to side of head. The figure used, with slight alterations, in the artist's second version of subject, circa 1848.

ILLUSTRATION: McDermott, p. 284 (no. 6).

REFERENCES: McDermott, pp. 57, 93, 114; Christ-Janer, p. 66.

44. Boatman: for *Boatmen on the Missouri*, 1846

Album no. ML95. 8¾ x 8½

Man standing, turned toward left, facing observer, holding a setting pole; *verso:* two heads of old men, left; landscape, right; three lines of MSS, top.

ILLUSTRATIONS: McDermott, p. 281 (no. 3) (*recto*); *George Caleb Bingham, Sesquicentennial Exhibition* . . . (The Nelson Gallery and Atkins Museum *Bulletin*, vol. III), p. [26] (*verso*).

REFERENCE: McDermott, p. 55.

45. Boatman: for *Boatmen on the Missouri*, 1846

Man in top hat, seated on plank, turned to right, looking out toward spectator. Inscribed and dated, *recto*, lower left: "G. G. [*sic*] Bingham, 1839." Inscribed on *verso:* "A Mississippi River Steamboat hand. Sketch by G. G. [*sic*] Bingham 1839. Very valuable. From collection of J. C. Maguire, Washington, D.C. Dec. 10–11, 1888 . . . ."

Pencil, brush and ink: 9½ x 8

E.M.B. Inscription on recto undoubtedly not in artist's hand, and dating indicated is obviously unreliable. James C. McGuire of Washington, D.C., was well known as a collector of American paintings and was an early collector of drawings by American artists. He owned at least one other drawing by Bingham which is now in the collection of the Museum of Fine Arts, Boston.

Lent by John S. Kebabian

46. Boatman: for *Lighter Relieving a Steamboat Aground*, 1847

Album no. ML46. 10⅝ x 8½

Man seated on barrel, facing right; right arm rests across right leg.

ILLUSTRATION: McDermott, p. 288 (no. 10).

REFERENCE: McDermott, p. 60.

47. Rapt Listener: for *Lighter Relieving a Steamboat Aground*, 1847

Album no. ML61. 10¾ x 8⅜

Man seated on box, facing observer; right arm rests on raised right knee, right hand covering lower part of face.

ILLUSTRATIONS: Christ-Janer, Figure 14; McDermott, p. 289 (no. 11)

REFERENCES: Christ-Janer, p. 47; McDermott, p. 60.

275–849 O—67——6

48. Card Player: for *Raftsmen Playing Cards*, 1847

Album no. ML4. 10¾ x 8⅜

Man seated, turned toward left, studying cards in his left hand. The same figure used by artist in second version of subject, *In a Quandary* or *Mississippi Raftmen at Cards*, 1851.

ILLUSTRATIONS: Rusk, Pl. XXIII, l.r.; Christ-Janer, Figure 8; McDermott, p. 295 (no. 17).

REFERENCES: Rusk, p. 42; Christ-Janer, p. 44; McDermott, p. 61.

49. Card Player: for *Raftsmen Playing Cards*, 1847

Album no. ML5. 10⅞ x 8⅝

Man seated, turned toward right, holding cards in his left hand. The same figure used by artist in second version of subject, *In a Quandary* or *Mississippi Raftmen at Cards*, 1851.

ILLUSTRATIONS: Rusk, Pl. XXIII, 1.1.; Christ-Janer, Figure 7; McDermott, p. 294 (no. 16).

REFERENCES: Rusk, p. 42; Christ-Janer, p. 43; McDermott, p. 61.

50. Raftman: for *Raftsmen Playing Cards*, 1847

Album no. ML6. 10¾ x 8⅜

Man standing, facing left in profile, bending forward. The same figure used by the artist in second version of subject, *In a Quandary* or *Mississippi Raftmen at Cards*, 1851. A variant of ML18 used in *The County Election* (1)(2), 1851–1852.

ILLUSTRATIONS: Christ-Janer, Figure 9; McDermott, p. 297 (no. 19).

REFERENCES: Christ-Janer, p. 44; McDermott, p. 61.

51. Raftman: for *Raftsmen Playing Cards*, 1847

Album no. ML63. 10⅞ x 8½

Man standing, facing observer, right leg raised and resting on barrel. The figure, adapted, with changes in costume, for *Jolly Flatboatmen in Port*, 1857. A variant of figure used in *The County Election* (1)(2), 1851/1852.

ILLUSTRATIONS: Christ-Janer, Figure 10; McDermott, p. 296 (no. 18).

REFERENCES: Christ-Janer, pp. 44–45; McDermott, p. 61.

52. Raftman Dozing: for *Raftsmen Playing Cards*, 1847
Album no. ML87. 9½ x 8½
Man seated on plank, facing the observer, sleeping; head resting against right hand; barefoot, right leg left unfinished. The figure used again in *Jolly Flatboatmen in Port*, 1857.

ILLUSTRATIONS: Rusk, Pl. XXII, top; McDermott, p. 298 (no. 20).

REFERENCES: Rusk, p. 42; McDermott, pp. 61, 124.

53. Elderly Spectator: for *The Stump Orator*, 1847
Album no. ML9. 9¾ x 11⅝
Man seated on ground, facing left, back turned partly toward observer.

ILLUSTRATION: McDermott, p. 309 (no. 31).

REFERENCE: McDermott, p. 67.

54. Political Opponent: for *The Stump Orator*, 1847
Album no. ML20. 11⅛ x 8⅜
Man seated, facing observer, whittling; two heads, upper right and left center; *verso:* sketch of left side of figure.

ILLUSTRATIONS: Rusk, Pl. XIV, u.r.; *Art Quarterly* (1957), p. 391, Figure 3; McDermott, p. 301 (no. 23).

REFERENCE: McDermott, pp. 53, 67, 113.

55. Spectator at Ease: for *The Stump Orator*, 1847

   Album no. ML36. 9⅝ x 12¼

   Young man reclining on ground, turned toward left, back to observer. The same figure used by the artist in *Stump Speaking*, 1853–1854.

   ILLUSTRATION: McDermott, p. 372 (no. 94).

   REFERENCE: McDermott, p. 109.

56. Patient Listener: for *The Stump Orator*, 1847

   Album no. ML43. 11⅛ x 8½

   Man seated on log, facing right, turned away from observer.

   ILLUSTRATION: McDermott, p. 307 (no. 29).

   REFERENCE: McDermott, p. 67.

57. Substantial Citizen: for *The Stump Orator*, 1847

   Album no. ML67. 12⅝ x 9½

   Man seated on log, facing left in profile; holds walking stick in right hand; *verso:* sketches of two heads, torso.

   ILLUSTRATIONS: Christ-Janer, Figure 53; *Art Quarterly* (1957), p. 393, Figure 7; McDermott, p. 306 (no. 28).

   REFERENCES: Christ-Janer, p. 83; McDermott, p. 67.

58. "Citizen of Undoubted Worth": for *The Stump Orator*, 1847

   Album no. ML70. 10⅜ x 8¼

   Man seated on log, turned toward left, legs crossed; hat in hand. The same model apparently used in ML80.

   ILLUSTRATIONS: Christ-Janer, Figure 13; *Art Quarterly* (1957), p. 394, Figure 10; McDermott, p. 304 (no. 26).

   REFERENCES: Christ-Janer, p. 47; McDermott, p. 67.

59. Serious Citizen: for *The Stump Orator*, 1847

Album no. ML80. 10¼ x 8½

Man seated on log, facing observer, looking out to left, right hand raised to chin; *verso*: sketch of left side of figure. Figure adapted, with slight alterations, in *Stump Speaking*, 1853/1854. The same model apparently used in ML70.

ILLUSTRATIONS: *Art Quarterly* (1957), p. 394, Figure 8; McDermott, p. 318 (no. 40).

REFERENCE: McDermott, p. 67.

60. Amused Spectator: for *The Stump Orator*, 1847

Album no. ML81. 10½ x 8⅜

Man seated on plank, facing observer, turned slightly to left, right arm resting on raised right knee. Sketch of right arm with gesturing hand, upper left. Figure adapted, with slight alteration, in *Stump Speaking*, 1853/1854.

ILLUSTRATIONS: *Art Quarterly* (1957), p. 392, Figure 4; McDermott, p. 320 (no. 42)

REFERENCE: McDermott, p. 67.

61. Village Character: for *The Stump Orator*, 1847

Album no. ML88. 10¼ x 6⅞

Three-quarter-length figure standing, facing observer, hands in pockets. The same figure used by the artist in *Stump Speaking*, 1853/1854.

ILLUSTRATIONS: Rusk, Pl. XXXII, l.r.; Christ-Janer, Figure 50; McDermott, p. 317 (no. 39).

REFERENCES: Rusk, p. 61; Christ-Janer, p. 81; McDermott, pp. 67, 109–110.

62. Boatman: for *Watching the Cargo*, 1849

Album no. ML48. 11 x 8⅝

Man seated on box, facing observer, legs crossed, smoking pipe. Figure also used in *Mississippi Boatman*, 1850.

ILLUSTRATIONS: Christ-Janer, Figure 23; McDermott, p. 337 (no. 59).

REFERENCES: Christ-Janer, p. 52; McDermott, p. 73.

63. Politician: possibly for *Country Politician*, 1849

Album no. ML65. 9⅝ x 9¼

Man seated in chair, turned toward left, gestures with hands. The figure adapted, with slight alterations, for *Canvassing for a Vote*, 1851/1852.

ILLUSTRATIONS: Christ-Janer, Figure 42; McDermott, p. 327 (no. 49).

REFERENCES: Christ-Janer, p. 70; McDermott, p. 72.

64. Woodboatman: for *The Wood-Boat*, 1850

Album no. ML101. 15¼ x 9⅜

Man standing, facing observer, leaning on pole; *verso:* sketch of upper part of figure. Figure used, with some alteration, in *Woodboatmen on a River*, 1854.

ILLUSTRATIONS: Museum of Modern Art, New York, *George Caleb Bingham* . . . (1935) (cover); *St. Louis Post-Dispatch*, July 1, 1951; McDermott, p. 343 (no. 65).

REFERENCE: McDermott, p. 77.

65. Old Settler: for *Shooting for the Beef*, 1850

Album no. ML96. 9⅛ x 6⅞

Old man standing, turned toward right, looking out to spectator, leans on walking stick with both hand. Possibly the same figure used, with alterations in pose of hands and costume, in *The Squatters*, 1850.

ILLUSTRATIONS: *Art Quarterly* (1956), p. 70, Figure 2; McDermott, p. 339 (no. 61).

REFERENCE: McDermott, pp. 75, 76.

66. Marksman: for *Shooting for the Beef*, 1850
Album no. ML100. 15¼ x 9¾
Man standing, turned slightly to left, facing observer; loading rifle.
ILLUSTRATION: McDermott, p. 338 (no. 60).
REFERENCE: McDermott, p. 75.

67. Pioneer (Flanders Callaway): for *The Emigration of Daniel Boone*, 1851
Album no. ML3. 14⅝ x 9⅝
Man walking toward observer, holding rifle; *verso:* sketch of arm.
ILLUSTRATIONS: Rusk, Pl. XXVI, top; Christ-Janer, Figure 27; McDermott, p. 348 (no. 70).
REFERENCES: Rusk, p. 52; Christ-Janer, p. 59; McDermott, p. 85.

68. Fisherman Waiting for a Bite: for *Fishing on the Mississippi*, 1851
Album no. ML50. 8⅞ x 11¼
Young man reclining on rock, facing right, right hand resting against chin; figure only partly shown. The figure used, with slight alterations, in *Jolly Flatboatmen in Port*, 1857.
ILLUSTRATIONS: Christ-Janer, Figure 26; McDermott, p. 347 (no. 69).
REFERENCES: Christ-Janer, p. 56; McDermott, p. 82.

69. Two Citizens: for *The County Election* (1)(2), 1851–1852
Album no. ML17. 13¾ x 10⅛
Two men conversing: figure at left facing right in profile, gesturing; figure at right facing observer.
ILLUSTRATIONS: Rusk, Pl. XXX, l.r.; Christ-Janer, Figure 39; McDermott, p. 365 (no. 87).
REFERENCES: Rusk, p. 57; Christ-Janer, p. 68; McDermott, p. 94.

70. Curious Citizen: for *The County Election* (1)(2), 1851–1852
Album no. ML 18. 11⅜ x 9
Man standing, facing left, bending forward. A variant of ML6 used in *Raftsmen Playing Cards*, 1847, and *In a Quandary*, 1851.
ILLUSTRATIONS: Christ-Janer, Figure 38; McDermott, p. 364 (no. 86).
REFERENCES: Christ-Janer, p. 68; McDermott, p. 94.

71. Boy Playing Mumble-the-Peg: for *The County Election* (1)(2), 1851–1852
Album no. ML25. 8⅞ x 10
Boy seated on ground, facing observer; partial sketch of another figure faintly visible, right.
ILLUSTRATIONS: Rusk, Pl. XXIX, top; Christ-Janer, Figure 31; McDermott, p. 351 (no. 73).
REFERENCES: Rusk, p. 57; Christ-Janer, p. 66; McDermott, p. 93.

72. Conscientious Voter: for *The County Election* (1)(2), 1851–1852
Album no. ML30. 11⅝ x 9
Man seated on steps, facing observer, making notes on writing pad resting on lap. The figure is a slight variant of that in the paintings.

ILLUSTRATIONS: Christ-Janer, Figure 37; McDermott, p. 363 (no. 85).
REFERENCES: Christ-Janer, p. 68; McDermott, p. 94.

73. Voter: for *The County Election* (1)(2), 1851–1852
Album no. ML40. 11½ x 8⅞
Man walking up steps, facing right, turned away from observer.
ILLUSTRATION: McDermott, p. 359 (no. 81).
REFERENCE: McDermott, pp. 52, 94.

74. Veteran of '76: for *The County Election* (1)(2), 1851–1852
Album no. ML49. 11⅝ x 9
Old man walking down steps, facing left, leaning heavily on long stick; numbers "76" appear on his hat.
ILLUSTRATIONS: Rusk, Pl. XXX, u.r.; Christ-Janer, Figure 36; McDermott, p. 360 (no. 82).
REFERENCES: Rusk, p. 57; Christ-Janer, p. 68; McDermott, p. 94.

75. Hearty Drinker: for *The County Election* (1)(2), 1851–1852
Album no. ML53. 11⅜ x 9⅛
Man seated on chair, facing observer, holds up glass in right hand which is being filled from bottle partly visible at upper left.
ILLUSTRATIONS: Christ-Janer, Figure 30; McDermott, p. 354 (no. 76).
REFERENCES: Christ-Janer, p. 66; McDermott, p. 93.

76. Two Citizens Conversing: for *The County Election* (1)(2), 1851–1852
Album no. ML82. 11½ x 9¼
Two men standing, one in foreground with back to observer, other turned toward observer, gesturing with hands.

ILLUSTRATIONS: Christ-Janer, Figure 35; *Art Quarterly* (1957) p. 394, Figure 8; McDermott, p. 358 (no. 80).
REFERENCES: Christ-Janer, pp. 67–68; McDermott, p. 94.

77. Negro Boy: for *The County Election* (1)(2), 1851–1852
Album no. ML86. 12¼ x 8¼

Negro boy stands in front of table, facing right in profile, pouring from jug. Bareheaded in sketch, wears hat in painted versions.
ILLUSTRATIONS: Rusk, Pl. XXX, 1.1.; Christ-Janer, Figure 29; City Art Museum of St. Louis, *Westward the Way*, 1954, Figure 151; McDermott, p. 353 (no. 75).
REFERENCES: Rusk, p. 57; Christ-Janer, pp. 65–66; McDermott, p. 93.

78. Politician: for *Stump Speaking*, 1853–1854
Album no. ML28. 11⅝ x 9⅝

Stump speaker, facing right, three-quarter figure; gestures with hands.
ILLUSTRATIONS: Rusk, Pl. XXXII, top; Christ-Janer, Figure 47; *Art Quarterly* (1957), p. 391, Figure 2; McDermott, p. 299 (no. 21).
REFERENCES: Rusk, p. 61; Christ-Janer, pp. 80–81; McDermott, pp. 67, 109.

79. Attentive Citizen: for *Stump Speaking*, 1853–1854
Album no. ML60. 12⅝ x 9⅝

Man seated, turned toward right, head turned to upper right; right arm rests across right leg.
ILLUSTRATIONS: Christ-Janer, Figure 45; McDermott, p. 370 (no. 92).
REFERENCES: Christ-Janer, p. 80; McDermott, p. 109.

80. Influential Citizen: for *Stump Speaking*, 1853–1854

Album no. ML64. 11⅞ x 9¾

Man seated on bench, turned toward right, holds walking stick in left hand.

ILLUSTRATIONS: Christ-Janer, Figure 44; McDermott, p. 368 (no. 90).

REFERENCES: Christ-Janer, pp. 79–80; McDermott, p. 109.

81. "Outstanding Citizen": for *Stump Speaking*, 1853–1854

Album no. ML79. 12⅜ x 10¼

Man seated, turned toward left, head shown almost in profile; legs crossed, wears top hat, holds walking stick in right hand.

ILLUSTRATIONS: Christ-Janer, Figure 52; *Art Quarterly* (1957), p. 392, Figure 5; McDermott, p. 373 (no. 95).

REFERENCES: Christ-Janer, p. 82; McDermott, p. 109.

82. Small Businessman: for *Stump Speaking*, 1853–1854

Album no. ML91. 10¾ x 9¼

Boy seated on ground, facing spectator, counting money in hand basket at side.

ILLUSTRATION: McDermott, p. 371 (no. 93).

REFERENCE: McDermott, p. 109.

83. "Aged Citizen"; for *Stump Speaking*, 1853–1854

Album no. ML99. 12½ x 9¾

Elderly man seated facing right, resting chin against head of walking stick; accompanied by dog.

ILLUSTRATIONS: Rusk, Pl XXXII, 1.1.; Christ-Janer, Figure 49; McDermott, p. 369 (no 91).

REFERENCES: Rusk, p. 61; Christ-Janer, p. 81; McDermott, p. 109.

84. Appreciative Listener

Album no. ML16. 12½ x 9½ (approx.)

Man seated on bench, facing observer, smiling; legs crossed, right hand raised to chin.

ILLUSTRATIONS: City Art Museum of St. Louis, *Westward the Way*, 1954, Figure 154; McDermott, p. 314 (no. 36).

REFERENCE: McDermott, p. 67.

85. Spectator

Album no. ML68. 8½ x 11

Man seated on ground, facing left in profile; right hand raised to chin. Related in pose to drawing in M. & M. Karolik Collection of American Drawings, Museum of Fine Arts, Boston.

ILLUSTRATIONS: Christ-Janer, Figure 22; McDermott, p. 312 (no. 34).

RÉFERENCES: Christ-Janer, p. 51; McDermott, p. 67.

86. Persuasive Speaker

Album no. ML75. 12½ x 9⅜

Man seated on bench, turned toward left, looking out to right, gesturing with right hand; holds top hat in left hand.

ILLUSTRATION: McDermott, p. 315 (no. 37).

REFERENCE: McDermott, p. 67.

Paintings by George Caleb Bingham referred to in the preceding catalog of drawings but not included in the present exhibition are: *Fur Traders Descending the Missouri*, coll: Metropolitan Museum of Art, New York, New York; *Trappers' Return*, coll: The Detroit Institute of Arts, Detroit, Michigan; *The Jolly Flatboatmen* (2), private collection; *The County Election* (1), coll: City Art Museum of St. Louis, St. Louis, Missouri; *The County Election* (2), coll: The Boatmen's National Bank, St. Louis, Missouri; *Raftsmen Playing Cards*, City Art Museum of St. Louis, St. Louis, Missouri; *The Stump Orator* (location unknown); *Stump Speaking*, coll: The Boatmen's National Bank, St. Louis, Missouri; *Watching the Cargo*, coll: State Historical Society of Missouri, Columbia, Missouri; *Country Politician*, (location unknown); *The Squatters*, private collection; *Fishing on the Mississippi*, coll: Nelson Gallery-Atkins Museum, Kansas City, Missouri; *Lighter Relieving Steamboat Aground*, private collection.

Chronology

1811 Born on plantation, Augusta County, Virginia, March 20.

1819 Family moved to Franklin, Howard County, Missouri.

1820 Father operated tavern in Franklin.

1821–1822 Father took partnership in tobacco factory in Franklin; was appointed judge of county court, Howard County, January 1821, and circuit court judge, 1822–1823.

1823 Father died December 26.

1827 Mother and children moved to farm near Arrow Rock, Saline County.

circa 1827–1832 In Boonville, circa 1827-1828, apprenticed to the Reverend Justinian Williams, cabinetmaker. Inspired by unknown itinerant portrait painter; decided to become painter during this period; painted signs and probably made early efforts at portraiture. Said to have attempted trip to St. Louis, about 1830, but turned back owing to illness.

circa 1833 Began career as portrait painter, probably at Arrow Rock.

1834–1835 In Columbia, portrait painting, until March 1835. Friendship with Major Rollins. In St. Louis by mid March. Afterward to Liberty, Clay County, portrait painting, contracted smallpox, remained until early June. Returned to St. Louis by late November.

1836 In St. Louis, probably until March. Married Sarah Elizabeth Hutchison in Boonville in April, returned to St. Louis by September. Winter in Natchez, Mississippi, painting portraits.

1837 In Natchez until about mid May. Returned to Missouri, in Boonville; summer in Columbia, painting portraits. Son Newton born March 26.

1838 Went to Philadelphia to study, between March and early June; may have also visited New York. Afterward paid short visit to Baltimore, probably returned to Missouri by early July. Exhibited "Western Boatmen Ashore" at Apollo Gallery, New York, fall show. Probably spent winter in Saline County, painting portraits.

1839 Still in Saline County, early in year. Returned to St. Louis by May.

1840 Sent six paintings to National Academy of Design, New York; address given as St. Louis. At Rocheport, Missouri, in June, attended convention in connection with presidential campaign, made political speech, reportedly painted campaign banners. In Washington, District of Columbia, by late December.

1841–1844 Washington, District of Columbia, portrait painting. In 1842 sent picture to National Academy exhibition. Visited exhibition in Philadelphia, painted portraits there, mid June 1843. Painted portrait of John Quincy Adams in Washington, May 1844. Spent six months in Petersburg, Virginia, during this period (1841). Son Newton died in Washington, March 13, 1841; another son, Horace, was born there, March 15, 1841. Returned to Boonville by September 1844, painted banners for national Whig convention. Late December in Jefferson City, studio in Capitol; painted portraits of governor and others there.

1845 In St. Louis, submitted first pictures to American Art-Union, New York, by late June: "Fur Traders Descending the Missouri," "The Concealed Enemy," and two landscapes. Daughter Clara born March 14.

1846 In Arrow Rock. Candidate for State Legislature from Saline County, nominated June 24; elected by small majority, August 14; election contested by opponent, E. D. Sappington, November 20; case decided in favor of Sappington, December 18. Submitted "The Jolly Flatboatmen" to American Art-Union; purchased October.

1847 Paintings "Lighter Relieving a Steamboat Aground" and "Raftsmen Playing Cards" on exhibition in St. Louis.

1848 In Arrow Rock. Nominated to represent Saline County in State Legislature, July; elected over Sappington, August. Death of Sarah Elizabeth Bingham at Arrow Rock, November 29. In Jefferson City, late December, named to Committee on Federal Relations. "Stump Orator" in National Academy of Design exhibition.

1849 In Jefferson City during January and February. In New York, July and August, submitted "Raftsmen on the Ohio," "Watching the Cargo," "St. Louis Wharf," "Country Politician," and "A Boatman" to American Art-Union. Afterward probably in Philadelphia. Three paintings, including "Feeding Time," purchased by Western Art Union, Cincinnati. In Columbia, painted portraits, late September. Married Eliza K. Thomas (second wife) at Columbia, December 2.

1850 In Columbia, late May; by July in St. Louis, where he painted "Shooting for the Beef." November in New York, submitted "The Squatters" and "The Wood-Boat" to American Art-Union. Probably sent two landscapes to Western Art Union, and two paintings, "Mississippi Boatman" and "Daybreak in a Stable," to Philadelphia Art Union at this time.

1851 Still in New York by late March, painted "Emigration of Daniel Boone" while there, and very probably "In a Quandary" Goupil & Co. Submitted "Trappers' Return" and "Fishing on the Mississippi" to American Art-Union. In St. Louis in May, on way home. By mid May in Columbia, evidently remained there until October, at work on "The County Election," "Candidate Electioneering" ("Canvassing for a Vote"), and other pictures. In St. Louis in November to spend winter.

1852 Remained in St. Louis probably through March, painted portraits. By April in Columbia. Went to Baltimore in June as delegate for Eighth District to Whig national convention; later in month in Philadelphia and New York, consulted with engravers for "The County Election." By November in Glasgow and St. Louis. Spent winter in St. Louis.

1853 Left St. Louis, March 10, for New Orleans, exhibited "The County Election" there and sold the picture. Returned to Kentucky and in May in Louisville and Lexington raised subscriptions for the engraving. By July had also visited Danville, Frankfort, Harrodsburg, and intended going to Paris and Richmond. During September in New York, visited exhibition of Industry of All Nations, then to Philadelphia. Began to paint "Stump Speaking" by early November; spent winter there superintending work on engraving by Sartain of "The County Election."

1854 Remained in Philadelphia, probably through mid July, with at least one short trip to New York. Completed "Stump Speaking" by early February; "The Verdict of the People" begun by late May. Returned to Missouri, probably to St.

275–849 O—67——7

Louis. In Columbia in September en route to Boonville, where he attended State Fair.

1855 Returned to Philadelphia by January. Late June in Independence, remained there at least until early August. "The Verdict of the People" completed at Philadelphia by late spring. Painted portraits in Columbia by September 14. At work on portraits in Jefferson City by November 14; remained until December, attending Whig meeting and making a speech in Capitol, December 1.

1856 Began painting "Washington Crossing the Delaware" in Columbia by March 14. In St. Louis during May, exhibited "The Verdict of the People." Commissioned by Missouri State Legislature to paint full-length portraits of Washington and Jefferson; June, July in Boston to copy portraits of subjects in connection with work. In Philadelphia in August. Sailed for Europe August 14; in Paris September 2. Arrived in Düsseldorf about November 1. Painting of portrait of Washington in progess during December.

1857 "The First Lesson in Music" in exhibition of Pennsylvania Academy of Fine Arts. At work in Düsseldorf; portrait of Washington completed during fall; afterward began portrait of Jefferson. Began work on "Jolly Flatboatmen in Port" before June, completed by late October.

1858 Completed portrait of Jefferson in Düsseldorf, probably during April.

1859 Returned to United States; in Washington, District of Columbia, served as member of convention of National Art Association meeting there, January 12–14. Later in month in Jefferson City, where he delivered portraits of Washington and Jefferson; afterward in Columbia. In February in St. Louis and again in

Jefferson City, where he was commissioned by State Legislature to execute portraits of Clay and Jackson, February 14. Remained in Jefferson City until mid March, painted portraits; then in Columbia and Kansas City. Went to Brunswick, Missouri, in April. Stopped off at St. Louis early in May on way to Washington and New York; then sailed for Europe. Commissioned to paint portrait of Humboldt for St. Louis Mercantile Library Association in May. Returned to Düsseldorf early in June, planned to go to Berlin to make studies for Humboldt portrait. Back in New York in September; by December in Jefferson City.

1860 First week of January in Washington, District of Columbia, painted portrait of Jackson after Sully in connection with State commission; also served again as member of National Art Association there, January 10, 12–13, as well as on a committee of conference of the House of Representatives. Returned to Missouri, in Columbia, early March. Delivered portrait of Humboldt to Mercantile Library, St. Louis, late April. Exhibited pictures at Pennsylvania Academy of Fine Arts, Philadelphia, and at Western Academy of Art, St. Louis. By mid September in Independence, painted portraits; had completed portrait of Jackson at Kansas City. Portrait of Clay finished by December, probably at Kansas City.

1861 Portraits of Clay and Jackson set up in House of Representatives at Jefferson City, January 7. Later in month in St. Louis to arrange for frames for portraits, exhibited them there as well, late February. Left March 6 for Houston, Texas, to settle estate of brother, Matthias A. Bingham, who had died January 12; returned to Kansas City by mid May. Appointed captain in U.S. Volunteer Reserve Corps in Kansas City during summer. Son James Rollins born September 21.

1862 Moved to Jefferson City, late January, having been appointed state treasurer, January 4; position held until 1865.

1863 Commissioned by Secretary of State of Missouri to paint a portrait of General Nathaniel Lyon, August 1. "General Order No. 11" issued by General Thomas Ewing in Kansas City. August 25.

1865 Completed term of office as state treasurer. Began to paint "Order No. 11" at Independence by November.

1866 In June a candidate for Congress from Sixth District, made speech at state convention. July in St. Louis. Painted "Major Dean in Jail."

1867 In Independence, completed portrait of General Lyon, late March.

1868 Chosen elector at Democratic state convention, late May. Completed "Order No. 11" in December.

1869 In Columbia, March. Elected school director at Independence, October. Death of son Horace.

1870 Painted second version of "Order No. 11" at Independence between March and April. Moved from Independence to Kansas City, May.

1871 In Jefferson City in January, exhibited portrait of General F. P. Blair. In Kansas City, March, at work on full-length portrait of Blair, completed by July. September in Columbia, at work on portrait of Major Rollins, commissioned for the University. November in Kansas City; by late December in Philadelphia in connection with engraving of "Order No. 11" then in progress by Sartain.

1872 Still in Philadelphia, late January; completed "Washington Crossing the Delaware," begun in 1856; plate of "Order No. 11" almost finished. May in Kansas City; July in Baltimore;

later in Denver, painted "View of Pike's Peak" by late October. By November had returned to Kansas City, at work on portraits.

1873 Completed full-length portrait of Rollins at Kansas City, late March. In Houston and then Austin, Texas, April, settling brother's estate. Returned to Kansas City, May. July in Marshall and Arrow Rock; August in Kansas City. Exhibited "Order No. 11" and "Washington Crossing the Delaware" at Louisville, Kentucky, Industrial Exposition, September; attended exposition and afterward back in Kansas City; at work on portraits by mid December.

1874 In Kansas City, painted portraits through winter. Appointed president of Kansas City Board of Police Commissioners. May 11. At work on portraits, June. A candidate for Congress from Eighth District, late July, but withdrew from list of candidates for nomination at Democratic convention in Kansas City, September. Almost completed "The Puzzled Witness," exhibited in St. Louis, December.

1875 Appointed adjutant-general of Missouri, January; by January 19 in Jefferson City. Made February report on Samuels case in Clay County.

1876 In Washington, District of Columbia, March and April in connection with disposition of war claims for state; painted portraits of Vinnie Ream and Florence Crittenden Coleman there. During May and June in Jefferson City; October in Fulton, where his wife was institutionalized. Death of Eliza Thomas Bingham at Fulton, November 3, after his return to Jefferson City.

1877 Authorized by State Legislature in March to paint historical picture of Jackson before Civil Court of Louisiana. In June, appointed professor of art of University of Missouri's newly established school of Art. From July to September in Boonville, painted portraits, afterward in Columbia. November in Kansas City.

1878 In St. Louis in January, and later in Kansas City. Between February and March in Washington, D.C., completed "The Jolly Flatboatmen" (3) and "Palm Leaf Shade," at work on "Little Red Riding Hood." In Columbia, and returned to Kansas City by late May. Married Mrs. Martha Livingston Lykins (third wife) in Kansas City, June 18; couple afterward in Denver. Appointed a commissioner of Robert E. Lee Monument Association, November 8; on way to Richmond by mid November for meeting of commissioners November 27, stopped off at Columbia and Boonville; in Columbia on return, November 29.

1879 In Kansas City. Visited Columbia late May, remained until July 5. Returned to home in Kansas City, died July 7.

After the artist's death

1890 September 20, death of (third) wife, Mrs. Martha Livingston Bingham, at Kansas City.

1893 March 25, administrator's sale of Bingham estate held at Findlay's Art Store, Kansas City.

1901 May 5. Death of daughter Clara (Mrs. Thomas Benton King) at Stephenville, Erath County, Texas.

1910 December 31, death of son, James Rollins Bingham.

Selected Bibliography

Books

Bingham, George Caleb. *An Address to the Public, Vindicating a Work of Art Illustrative of the Federal Military Policy in Missouri During the Late Civil War. By the Artist* . . . . Kansas City, Missouri, 1871.

Bloch, E. Maurice. *George Caleb Bingham: The Evolution of an Artist* and *Catalogue Raisonné*. Berkeley and Los Angeles, California, University of California Press, 1967.

Christ-Janer, Albert. *George Caleb Bingham of Missouri: The Story of an Artist* . . . New York, Dodd, Mead, 1940

Larkin, Lew. *Bingham: Fighting Artist. The Story of Missouri's Immortal Painter, Patriot, Soldier and Statesman* . . . St. Louis, Missouri, State Publishing Co. [1955]

McDermott, John Francis. *George Caleb Bingham, River Portraitist*. Norman, Oklahoma, University of Oklahoma Press [1959].

Rusk, Fern Helen. *George Caleb Bingham: The Missouri Artist* . . . Jefferson City Missouri, The Hugh Stephens Co., 1917.

Articles

American Art-Union. "The Gallery—No. 4" (Biography of Bingham). *Bulletin*, vol. II (August 1849), pp. 10–12.

American Art-Union. "New Work by Bingham." *Bulletin*, Series for 1850 (July 1850), pp. 64–65.

American Art-Union. "Mr. Bingham the Western Artist." *Bulletin*, Series for 1850 (December 1850), p. 157.

Bender, J. H. "Catalogue of Engravings and Lithographs After George C. Bingham." *The Print Collector's Quarterly*, vol. XXVII (February 1940), pp. 106–108.

"Bingham." *Western Journal*, vol. VII (1851), p. 45.

Bloch, E. Maurice. "Art in Politics." *Art in America*, vol. XXXIII (April 1945) pp. 93–100.

Bloch, E. Maurice. "George Caleb Bingham and His Landscape 'Method'." *Corcoran Gallery of Art Bulletin*, vol. XIII (October 1963), pp. 3–9.

"George Caleb Bingham, an Early Painter of Missouri." *Art World*, vol. III (November 1917), pp. 94–98.

Hall, Virginius C. "George Caleb Bingham, the Missouri Artist." *The Print Collector's Quarterly*, vol. XXVII (February 1940) pp. 9–25.

McDermott, John Francis. "The Quandary About Bingham's 'In a Quandary' and 'Raftmen Playing Cards'." *Bulletin of the City Art Museum of St. Louis*, vol. XLII (1957), pp. 6–9.

"Missouri History as Illustrated by George C. Bingham." *Missouri Historical Review*, vol. I (April 1907), pp. [181]–190.

[Parsons, Helen R.] "Missouri's Greatest Painter, George C. Bingham (1811–1879)." *Kansas City* [Missouri] *Public Library Quarterly*, vol. I (July 1901), pp. 65–68.

Penn, Dorothy. "George Caleb Bingham's 'Order No. 11'." *Missouri Historical Review*, vol. XL (April 1946), pp. 349–357.

Philadelphia Art Union. *Reporter*, vol. I (1851–1852).

Powell, Mary M. "George Caleb Bingham." *Bulletin of the City Art Museum of St. Louis*, vol. IX (October 1924), pp. 57–62.

Richardson, Edgar P. " 'Checker Players' by George Caleb Bingham." Detroit Institute of Arts Bulletin, vol. XXXII (1952–53), pp. 14–17; *Art Quarterly*, vol. XV (Autumn 1952), pp. 251–256.

Richardson, Edgar P. " 'The Trappers' Return' by George Caleb Bingham." *Detroit Institute of Arts Bulletin*, vol. XXX (1950–1951), pp. 81–84; reprinted *Art Quarterly*, vol. XIV (1951), pp. 78, 79, 81, 83.

Rollins, Curtis Burnam, ed. "Letters of George Caleb Bingham to James S. Rollins." *Missouri Historical Review*, vol. XXXII (October 1937–July 1938), pp. 3–34, 164–202, 340–377, 484–522; vol. XXXIII (October 1938 July 1939), pp. 45–78, 203–229, 349–384, 499–526.

Rollins, Curtis Burnam. "Some Recollections of George Caleb Bingham." *Missouri Historical Review*, vol. XX (July 1926), pp. 463–484.

Shapley, Fern Helen (Rusk). "Bingham's 'Jolly Flatboatmen'." *The Art Quarterly*, vol. XVII (Winter 1954), pp. 352–356.

Simonds, May. "A Pioneer Painter." *American Illustrated Methodist Magazine*, vol. VIII (October 1902), pp. 71–78.

Taggart, Ross E. " 'Canvassing for a Vote' and Some Unpublished Portraits by Bingham." *The Art Quarterly*, vol. XVIII (Autumn 1955), pp. 229–240.

Wadsworth Atheneum. *Bulletin*, Series 2, Number, 33 (May 1952), p. 3.

Catalogs

An Exhibition of the Work of George Caleb Bingham, 1811–1879, "The Missouri Artist." April, 1934, City Art Museum of St. Louis, Missouri, *Bulletin of the City Art Museum of St. Louis*, vol. XIX no. 2

Musick, James B., Arthur Pope, and Meyric R. Rogers. *George Caleb Bingham; The Missouri Artist, 1811–1879.* January 30–March 7, 1935, New York, The Museum of Modern Art.

Special Exhibition of the Paintings of George Caleb Bingham "The Missouri Artist," April nine to twenty-four, Nineteen hundred ten. In the Museum of Classical Archæology of the University of Missouri. University of Missouri, Columbia, Missouri, 1910.

Taggart, Ross E. *George Caleb Bingham, Sesquicentennial Exhibition, 1811–1961.* March 16–April 30, 1961, Kansas City, Missouri, William Rockhill Nelson Gallery of Art and Mary Atkins Museum of Fine Arts (May 16–June 30, 1961, St. Louis, Missouri, City Art Museum of St. Louis), *The Nelson Gallery and Atkins Museum Bulletin*, vol. III no. 3.

U.S. GOVERNMENT PRINTING OFFICE : 1967—O—275-849